Where the Action Is

WHERE THE ACTION IS

by
Randal Earl Denny

Beacon Hill Press of Kansas City
Kansas City, Missouri

ISBN: 0-8341-0723-6
Printed in the
United States of America

Cover by: Royce Ratcliff

Dedication

To my lifelong friends,
Robert Earls and Ron Jeffries
Brothers through sorrow and joy
with whom I have shared
many miles and
many songs

Contents

Foreword

The Book of Acts is indeed a book of action. Randal Denny brings into focus the action and the meaning of the acts.

He brings in each event a relevant truth and gives interesting incidents from life which relate to the act—its reason for happening and our profitable lesson from it.

It was in the Book of Acts that the Church took on its human form and processes. Those noble people who launched the world's greatest redemptive institution are clearly portrayed by Randal Denny. In this book, the Book of Acts moves afresh, speaking to us today.

This interesting writer captures truth and enlivens it in his own style. Read it. You will enjoy it. And the action of the great book herein portrayed will inspire you to promote the great cause afresh.

V. H. LEWIS

Acknowledgments

The warmhearted congregation in San Luis Obispo, affectionately called "Naz" by students of Cal Poly State University, inspires any pastor to study and preach. With a Bible on one knee and a notebook on the other, they are eager to learn. What a joy to walk with them through the pages of the Book of Acts!

Appreciation is hereby expressed for permission to quote from copyrighted materials as follows:

Abingdon Press: George Arthur Buttrick, ed., *The Interpreter's Bible*, vol. 9; Lyle Schaller, *The Decision-Makers*.

Back to the Bible Publishers: *Nuggets of Good News*.

Beacon Hill Press of Kansas City: Robert E. Maners, "Growing Pains," *Preacher's Magazine*, November, 1977.

Broadman Press: C. Roy Angell, *God's Gold Mines*.

Foundation for Christian Living: Norman Vincent Peale, *Favorite Stories of Positive Faith*.

Fleming H. Revell Co.: Charles L. Allen, *Prayer Changes Things*; Louis H. Evans, *Life's Hidden Power*.

Tyndale House Publishers: William F. Kerr, gen. ed., *Ministers' Research Service*.

Westminster Press: William Barclay, *Fishers of Men*; William Barclay, *The Acts of the Apostles*, The Daily Study Bible Series.

Word Books, Publishers: Clyde E. Fant, Jr., and William M. Pinson, Jr., *Twenty Centuries of Great Preaching*, vol. 10.

Zondervan Publishing House: Stuart Briscoe, *Living Dangerously*.

I owe a great debt to my wife, Ruth. She has had the same pastor for more than 20 years—and without complaint. She gives counsel, encouragement, and an attentive ear. With joy I have been nourished at her table. Faithfully she has applied her craft as chef. In these pages I have attempted to apply the craft of nourishment for her—and my people. It is imperative for me to serve the strong meat of God's Word.

RANDAL EARL DENNY
Church of the Nazarene
San Luis Obispo, Calif.

Introduction

The Book of Acts does not sit on the shelf well. Unlike a book of philosophy, it is a book of action! The Book of Acts doesn't even sound like a theological statement. It is the action-packed, bold march of Spirit-filled, Spirit-guided men. This book of high adventure even bristles with murders, attempted murders, intrigue, and escape. The dull-eyed, yawning scholar will sit right up on the edge of the chair! Luke has portrayed the Spirit-endued life as "where the action is."

Preachers and teachers enjoy debating the title of The Acts. Some are convinced it should be "The Acts of the Apostles," while others insist on "The Acts of the Holy Spirit."

I believe it is both—The Acts of the Apostles and the Holy Spirit—inevitably so, inseparably so. The actions of the apostles without the Spirit become manipulation and delusion. The story would lack love. The Holy Spirit without the actions of men becomes mysterious and vague. The story would lack life. Reading The Acts, one senses that God and man are going somewhere together. The heart of man is saturated with the Spirit of God. The result is not magic nor humanism, but the beautiful harmony of God and man. We are co-workers with Him.

Acts 5—8 portrays the working relationship of the Holy Spirit and Christ's people. Obviously, the Holy Spirit acts mightily—initiating and empowering. In response, His men are men of action—willingly and enthusiastically. Acts 5—8 is living proof that people gather "where the action is." I pray that as you read these pages, you will walk, listen, and live where the action is.

1

The Disciple
Who Flunked

Acts 4:34—5:11

A little boy fell out of bed. His mother came running to see what had happened. After she tucked him under the covers and kissed him, she asked, "How did you happen to fall out?"

"Oh," he replied, "I guess I went to sleep too near where I got in!"

That's the tragic story of Ananias and his wife, Sapphira. Somehow, someway they lost that oneness with the believers and, spiritually, went to sleep too near where they got in. Ananias was the disciple who flunked his course on discipleship.

In the early chapters of the Book of Acts, the "first things" of the Early Church are encountered: the first impact of the Spirit upon the believers, the first sermon of the Church, the first miracle of grace, the first opposition, the first revival, and now, the first internal crisis. Internal betrayal always wreaks more havoc than external persecution. Vance Havner says, "The church is never harmed half so much by woodpeckers on the outside as by termites on the inside!" Interestingly, this first defection from the church was not over theology, but stewardship!

Luke, having written about the great revival, went back and picked up the theme of "possessions with a purpose": "There were no needy persons among them. For from time to time those who owned lands or houses sold them, brought the money from the sales and put it at the apostles' feet, and it was distributed to anyone as he had need" (Acts 4: 34-35).

To illustrate the spontaneity of the Holy Spirit, Luke singles out one example of the loving generosity: "Joseph, a Levite from Cyprus, whom the apostles called Barnabas (which means Son of Encouragement), sold a field he owned and brought the money and put it at the apostles' feet" (vv. 36-37). Like the apostle Matthew, Barnabas left all to follow Christ! No doubt such an act of generosity caught the special notice of everyone in their fellowship. It was a beautiful, selfless demonstration of his sincerity and the profound conviction of his call from God. Though he had possessions, Barnabas didn't go away sorrowful like the rich young ruler who had left Jesus earlier. Barnabas made available whatever he had to those in need—a magnanimous gesture of love.

However, Luke is reminded of the tragic contrast by the disciple who flunked his course on discipleship. Luke introduces him: "Now a man named Ananias, together with his wife Sapphira, also sold a piece of property. With his wife's full knowledge he kept back part of the money for himself, but brought the rest and put it at the apostles' feet.

"Then Peter said, 'Ananias, how is it that Satan has so filled your heart that you have lied to the Holy Spirit and have kept for yourself some of the money you received for the land? Didn't it belong to you before it was sold? And after it was sold, wasn't the money at your disposal? What made you think of doing such a thing? You have not lied to men but to God'" (Acts 5:1-4).

What a contrast to Barnabas! Ananias had a good name,

meaning, "God is gracious!" His opportunities were just as great as those of Barnabas. His ministry could have been just as rewarding. From any indication it seems he loved Jesus, too, or he would not have been with the other believers.

An unknown author penned it clearly:

> Simply because a man falls in love with his wife, it does not mean that he is a good husband. To be a good husband requires study of a wife's interests, imagination to anticipate her needs, sympathethic insight to understand her unspoken wishes. Likewise, simply to say, "I love Jesus," does not mean that one is a Christian. Jesus said, "Take my yoke upon you, and learn of me." It is not enough merely to "come to Jesus"; we must go with Jesus and learn what He would have us do. Being a Christian involves the mind as well as the heart.

Somehow Ananias didn't learn enough about Jesus and about himself. Under the tests of the inner man, Ananias flunked the course on discipleship. Ananias earned three unforgettable Fs as a disciple.

I. Ananias Failed the Church

When the Church really needed men to stand true, he failed miserably.

Ananias failed the Church by *misconstruing his mission.* Called to glorify Jesus, he settled for trying to get glory for himself. Apparently the praise of people over Barnabas' gift was too much for him. He wanted the praise for giving all, when in reality he kept back money secretly. His love for God was weaker than his love for money and praise. Ananias wanted prestige without the price; he wanted full credit from partial contribution.

Billy Graham, the object of much publicity, warned: "God will not share His glory with anyone!"

Ananias failed the Church by *misrepresenting his commitment.* He had not sinned by bringing only part of

17

the money from the sale. He sinned by pretending it was the whole amount. Surely, people would attribute to him a reputation for generosity and total commitment! But his act of hypocrisy was his great sin.

Nothing brought more scorching words from Jesus than His severe attacks against hypocrisy. Jesus Christ was infinitely patient with sinners who were honest before God, but play-actors of righteousness stirred His emotions.

In appearing totally committed to God, Ananias was living a lie. Myron Augsburger wrote: "One who lies to the Holy Ghost is deliberately defending his sinful act or position. There is a vast difference between sin in which one is 'overtaken in a fault' (Gal. 6:1) and premeditated sin. The sin of lying to the Holy Ghost is a deliberate act of self-defense and self-justification before His call to holiness. Such sin is an expression of man's basic sin problem, that of revolting against God."[1]

Yes, Ananias was trying to keep face without keeping faith! In the sweet atmosphere of a genuine, Holy Ghost revival, he settled for an outward conformity without inner commitment to God.

Ananias failed the Church by *mishandling his sacred trust.* As he came and laid his offering at the feet of the apostles, he was reflecting an ancient legal method of transfering property by placing the deed at the feet of the new trustee or owner. When Ananias placed the partial price at Peter's feet, Peter responded with questions which underlined the fact that nothing is wrong with private ownership. He could have kept it all and still have been a disciple. If one is God's child, every bit of his possessions belong to God anyway. The Christian's role is to be a steward of God's property, and he is answerable to God alone.

However, Ananias failed in his sacred trust as a steward: "he kept back part of the money for himself" (Acts 5:2). That's the heart of bad stewardship—holding back what God tells one to give. One's sin is not in what he gives, but in what he holds back, what he keeps for himself.

Greek scholars Lake and Cadbury inform us that the word meaning "kept back" is used in classical Greek and carries the idea "(a) that the theft is secret; (b) that part of a larger quantity is (removed) . . . (c) it is to be noted . . . that the verb is less commonly used of theft from one individual by another than of taking to oneself . . . what is handled as a trust."[2] It is just plain embezzlement!

Whereas Jesus Christ emptied himself of riches for our sakes, the Early Church was inspired to set aside riches for Christ's sake. But Ananias and Sapphira embezzled from their sacred trust. When Luke used the term "kept back," he used the same word as the Greek version of Josh. 7:1 describing the sin of Achan during the fall of Jericho. Achan kept back gold and rich garments for himself during the siege of Jericho when God had commanded them to destroy everything. F. F. Bruce wrote: "The story of Ananias is to the book of Acts what the story of Achan is to the book of Joshua. In both narratives an act of deceit interrupts the victorious progress of the people of God."[3]

There is so much withholding from God in our money, our time, and our ministry to one another. What little is left over is squeezed out for God's use. How unfaithful many people are to God's sacred trust!

The Jews of Jesus' day gave not only a tithe, which is 10 percent of one's income, but several other offerings often amounting up to 30 percent for God's work. Americans, the wealthiest nation of the world today, give less than 2 percent of their income for God's work and charities—and keep more than 98 percent for themselves.

If the Holy Spirit revives His people in our day, they will never be satisfied with fellowshipping as a body just one hour per week—if it doesn't rain or if nothing else is

19

happening! The Church of Jesus Christ suffers because so many have failed to give it high priority.

II. Ananias Fumbled His Opportunity

With so many possibilities for service, Ananias fumbled God-given opportunity. Opportunities rarely knock us down. They simply present themselves, and it's up to us to make them exciting by our response.

Ananias fumbled his opportunity *to help people in need.* As the Church grew, many poor and needy people found a fellowship of love. Where else would they be considered as something of worth? So, inspired by the Spirit, the believers served Christ by helping people in need. We must learn to give that others might live!

Gen. Douglas MacArthur asked for 3,000 missionaries to come help fill Japan's theological vacuum after the emperor declared he was not divine. America sent only 124 missionaries. Dr. Louis Evans well described the dilemma:

> When we do not send over a $5,000 missionary to change the thinking of a nation, it seems we must eventually send over a $50,000 marine. We take our choice. Either we build a $10,000 chapel to teach a nation the love of God, or we must spend $10,000,000 on a naval vessel to avoid the results of their hate. It will be a thrilling day when America reaches the place where she knows how to spend her money; when we can shift the major emphasis from the military to the missionary. Our boys will go abroad, either today with God, or tomorrow with a gun—but they always go. You will have to make the choice.[4]

The president of a great university had these words placed under the glass top of his desk: "God gave us two ends to use; one to think with and the other to sit with. The future depends on which end we use—heads we win, tails we lose!" Let's not fumble our opportunity to help people in need.

20

Ananias fumbled the opportunity *to demonstrate his love for God*. His act of giving could have been a beautiful expression of his love for God. The Christian community, in a spirit of oneness, says, "What is mine is yours; I'll share it." It is a voluntary demonstration of love. And our self-giving to the fellowship of grace is one way of showing our love for God.

Ananias fumbled his opportunity *to trust God completely*. Perhaps he was fearful of going all the way with this new movement. By holding back some of the price of the land, they weren't willing to trust God completely for the future! They were trying to serve God and Mammon—but divided loyalty never works. A half cross is more difficult to carry than a whole cross. Poor Ananias was not at home with the world or with Christ.

We must face the facts of history. We are going to bear one cross or another—either the cross of war or the cross of Jesus. We are free to choose, but we will pay for one or the other.

A woman went to a plastic surgeon and asked, "What would it cost to have my face lifted?" When the doctor gave the estimate, she sadly replied, "That's too much! I'll just let the matter drop!"

Our old world needs to be lifted by the Good News, but it will cost us something to do it! We can't afford to let the matter drop. We must count on God to help us as we give our all to Him.

Ananias fumbled his opportunity *to have God's special blessing*. Had he given all, as he pretended to do, God would have kept His promise to pour out on him blessings which he could not contain. But he lost that golden opportunity. It could have been an act of love that triggered a fruitful response in others—but it withered on the ground.

An old man came to the studio of Rossetti, the great British artist. Bringing some of his own paintings, he asked the great artist to give his candid opinion. Sympathetically, Rossetti confessed he did not see much worth in the pictures—even though he tried not to offend the old man.

Then the visitor spread out another group of sketches which were the works of a youthful artist. Immediately Rossetti recognized the great talent behind those paintings and commented that the young artist could very well achieve greatness.

The old man said with a note of sadness: "Sir, I was that student!"

Opportunity was neglected and lost forever. And that's how Ananias fumbled so badly. How about us? How many of God's blessings have we forfeited by halfhearted discipleship in a day which demands our total commitment and full surrender to Christ!

Ananias got a third F. He not only *failed* the Church and *fumbled* his opportunity, but—

III. ANANIAS FORGOT GOD

[Peter said to him,] "You have not lied to men but to God."

When Ananias heard this, he fell down and died. And great fear seized all who heard what had happened. Then the young men came forward, wrapped up his body, and carried him out and buried him.

About three hours later his wife came in, not knowing what had happened. Peter asked her, "Tell me, is this the price you and Ananias got for the land?"

"Yes," she said, "that is the price."

Peter said to her, "How could you agree to test the Spirit of the Lord? Look! The feet of the men who buried your husband are at the door, and they will carry you out also."

At that moment she fell down at his feet and died. Then the young men came in and, finding her dead, carried her out and buried her beside her husband (Acts 5:4-10).

That tragic couple thought more of men's approval than God's. But Peter insisted they had lied to God, not men. While sin may hurt other people, sin is rebellion against God. King David admitted it when he exclaimed: "Against you, you only, have I sinned and done what is evil in your sight" (Ps. 51:4). While God is love, He is not to be fooled with. One must never neglect the note of warning for those who take God lightly. Ananias, like many today, tried to see how far one can go and not provoke God's wrath! Let me say emphatically—I want to be as far from that borderline as possible!

Ananias forgot that God's sight is sure. The attempt to deceive was a willful transgression. The sin of insincerity could not fool the blazing eye of God. He could see through it all. J. W. Goodwin wrote: "God has many ways of detecting hypocrisy. It is much harder to be a successful hypocrite than a successful Christian. The Christian has God on his side, while the hypocrite is dodging here and there for fear he will be found out. He lives in constant fear that his mask of profession will slip aside and his real condition will be known. There is no gain in dishonesty (with God). Judas did not spend the 30 pieces of silver. Ananias kept back a part, but lost what he sought to gain."[5]

While our secret holding back is a respectable sin among men, God views such covetousness along with the worst sins: "Do not be deceived: Neither the sexually immoral nor idolaters nor adulterers nor male prostitutes nor homosexual offenders nor thieves *nor the greedy* nor drunkards nor slanderers nor swindlers will inherit the kingdom of God" (1 Cor. 6:9-10). As Augsburger wrote: "We have the privilege of being honest before God voluntarily or being exposed by God involuntarily."[6] God knows our hearts.

Ananias forgot that God's Lordship is complete or not at all. One cannot settle for a commitment made a few years ago. A past response, however great, does not substitute for one's relationship of full surrender right now. Ananias forgot that his spiritual response at Pentecost or since was not sufficient for a surrendered heart at the present. The fellow who tries to hold back on God shall lose in the end.

As a result of the Christian missionaries meeting the Franks, many of the pagan chieftains and their warriors were baptized en masse. However, many of the warriors waded into the river to be immersed, but would hold their right hands, grasping battle-axes, above their heads, out of the water. The tribesmen went right on fighting and ransacking villages just as they had done before. They rationalized that their fighting arms and weapons had never been baptized! But Jesus is not Lord at all until He is Lord of all—until He has all of us!

Ananias forgot that God's judgment is final. Here is a warning—God is not mocked! Peter gave Sapphira a chance to confess, but she lied against the Holy Spirit just as her husband did—and God's judgment is irrevocable! It is spiritual suicide to ignore God's judgments. God will forgive those who start late in life to serve Him, but He will not forgive those who quit early!

God's judgment came to them in sudden death! While we know God is patient with sinners and is not willing that any should perish, it seems His punishment of Ananias and Sapphira was severe. However, since they were the first hypocrites in the Church, God demonstrated His wrath vividly as a warning for the generations who would follow. Throughout the Scriptures, the first offense of God's serious laws was punished by death so that all would know exactly His judgment against the sin.

Paul spoke of some of these representative punishments by death: "These things happened to them as examples and were written down as warnings for us, . . . So, if you think you are standing firm, be careful that you don't fall!" (1 Cor. 10:11-12).

Both Ananias and Sapphira were carried out. They weren't put out while they were alive, but carried out when they were dead. Unfortunately, they had first died inside! It didn't happen in a moment; they died gradually in their souls as they pulled away from God and sought something else to take His place.

God's judgment caused great fear. While miracles of mercy had caught the wonder of the crowds, this miracle of judgment had a sobering effect on all who heard about it. The believers were struck with an awe of God's judgments. It was a wholesome, godly fear which caused each one to examine his own soul: "Search me, O God, and know my heart; test my thoughts. Point out anything you find in me that makes you sad, and lead me along the path of everlasting life" (Ps. 139:23-24, TLB).

Jesus pointed out in a parable that there are tares among the wheat. The Church is not a perfect field. But there's coming a day of harvest in which God's judgments will separate the weeds from the good grain.

What happened to Ananias and Sapphira produced a great fear which served as a protection to the purity of the Church. Luke says, "No one else dared join them, even though they were highly regarded by the people. Nevertheless, more and more men and women believed in the Lord and were added to their number" (Acts 5:13-14). There's the difference between revival through human effort and revival which comes from the Spirit of God. The church needs to be so on fire that men would not join until they have been born again, added to the Lord first! Only then are they fit to be members! We don't need any more deadbeat church members whose prayers are empty words and whose testimonies have no ring of reality. We don't need halfhearted disciples of Jesus who are already dead on the

25

inside. We're too busy trying to bring in the newborn to waste time carrying out the spiritually dead! Let the dead bury the dead!

William Barclay put it well:

> In too many of the church's members there tends to be interest without commitment. . . . But there is all the difference in the world between enlisting in an Army and joining a club. If a man enlists in the Army, he accepts an obedience and a discipline which are absolute; he submits his will to higher authority; he abandons the right to run his own life and to make his own decisions. On the other hand, when a man joins a club he can go to it when he likes and he can stay away when he likes; he can give it as much or as little of his life and his time as he likes; he can play as much or as little a part in its activities as he wishes. He has no really binding obligation to it. There are too many Christians for whom membership of the Church is far more like joining a club than it is like enlisting in an Army.
>
> If we are interested in Jesus Christ it means that He is one of the competing interests in life; if we are committed to Him it means that He is the dominant dynamic of life—and nothing else will really do.[7]

One soon tires of pretending to be something he is not. When he dies, all that he had will belong to someone else. What one is he will keep! God sees in us and through us, and we must answer to Him alone.

Some folks have had that "Ananias spirit" of dishonesty, making a pretense of being totally committed—but dishonest in their homes, in their businesses, in their morals, in their values. No, people who are living a lie to the Holy Spirit aren't falling down dead—but many are walking around dead! Dead, empty hearts full of dead men's bones! The "Ananias spirit" and the Holy Spirit cannot occupy and live in the same heart. The only way back is rugged, open honesty with God! Let each one get down to

26

business and be honest with God. Whatever He says, one must obey!

Elisha A. Hoffman puts the challenge well:

Is your all on the altar of sacrifice laid?
  Your heart does the Spirit control?
You can only be blest and have peace and sweet rest
  As you yield Him your body and soul.[8]

2

God's Touch
of Wholeness

Acts 5:12-16

One man noted, "Get-well cards have become so humorous that if you don't get sick, you're missing half the fun."

The ministry of medicine which is so vital has become preponderous. The scope of medical knowledge has brought cures today for illnesses no one ever heard of a few years ago. With its development, modern medicine has become a multi-billion-dollar business, producing millions of miles of red tape. It has become so specialized today that if a head cold moves into one's chest, he has to change doctors!

A wife giving her husband a large dose of medicine commented: "It's an old cold remedy of my grandmother's. It may not cure what ails you, but it will make you think twice before you get sick again!"

Every church has felt the effects of widespread virus, creating vacancies in choirs, Sunday School teachers, ushers, and pulpits. With the help of modern technology, science should begin to find something to combat the virus—or, so I thought until I read: "Virus is a Latin word doctors use which means: 'Your guess is as good as mine!'"

After the tragic failure of Ananias and Sapphira, the

Church went through a period of purging. Outsiders had a great awe of the Church, not daring to join unless they were genuinely converted and committed to the Lord Jesus Christ. During this time, however, many sick people were wonderfully healed as the life of Jesus was being lived out through His people.

From Jesus' own ministry in Galilee as well as from the Holy Spirit's work through Jesus' followers after the Resurrection and Ascension, four important facts emerge concerning divine healing:

The first fact is that Jesus indisputably made sick people well. . . .

Second, He often made people well before He made them good. . . . "And everywhere He went, into villages, towns or countryside, they placed the sick in the market-places. They begged Him to let them touch even the edge of His cloak, and all who touched Him were healed" (Mark 6:56).

Third, when He gave His credentials to those who came from John the Baptist to ask if He were the Messiah or not, notice the order in which He listed them. "The blind receive sight, the lame walk, those who have leprosy are cured, the deaf hear, the dead are raised, and the good news is preached to the poor" (Matt. 11:5).

[Fourth] When He sent out His disciples, He gave them orders to do the selfsame thing. "And He sent them out to preach the kingdom of God and to heal the sick" (Luke 9:2).[1]

Any reading of Jesus' life and ministry gives the impression that He was One who could and did make people well. He did not say that disease is unreal or that it is always curable! And it is dangerous for the Church today to dodge the issue of divine healing.

C. William Fisher said in a sermon:

Probably no other teaching in the Bible has been questioned or criticized or ridiculed more than the teaching of divine healing.

29

Some have questioned out of a sincere quest for truth; others have criticized out of arrogant ignorance; while others have cynically ridiculed all religious healing as superstition or as a "religious racket."

Most churches, and most ministers—and I am afraid I am one—have been remiss in their responsibilities and privileges to proclaim a gospel for the *whole* man because they have been scared or sickened by the extremism of some who were apparently more interested in sensationalism and money than in a sane and meaningful ministry.[2]

Acts 5:12-16 is highlighted by people being restored to wholeness. The Bible teaches three basic things about God's plan for restoration of wholeness to man as seen in this passage.

I. Wholeness Is God's Ideal

Luke the physician noted: "The apostles performed many miraculous signs and wonders among the people" (Acts 5:12). "Miraculous signs"—not just miracles, but signs! The unusual happenings and healings were signs of something greater yet! Miracles were always signs or lessons of something far more important. The healings were signs of God's ideal for man as wholeness!

God does not want people to be crippled, nor does He take pleasure in their illnesses. His ideal is wholeness, completeness. As in the spiritual realm, God's ideal is often hampered by some of the scars of our fallen race. In life's situations which are far below God's ideal, He grieves also. As amazing as He is, God can often help people make the most of situations which are less than His ideal.

As I see it, divine healing is included in the atonement of Jesus on the Cross. Isaiah had prophesied: "Surely he took up our infirmities and carried our sorrows . . . he was pierced for our transgressions, he was crushed for our iniquities . . . and by his wounds we are healed" (Isa. 53:

30

4-5). The work of the Atonement is a reconciliation between God and man. When man is restored to God, his whole personality is affected—including body and soul. Jesus makes it clear that sickness is not a part of the divine order. God wants people not just well, but whole. He is most concerned about the total picture—a restoration of wholeness in His relationship with His children.

Jesus was not deterred from His healing ministry by religious laws of His day which forbid healing on the Sabbath Day. The Master also instructed His men to extend healing wherever they went.

God's ideal is not always effected in the lives of men. When Jesus went to His hometown, He was rejected by the people. The King James Version puts it graphically: "And he did not many mighty works there because of their unbelief" (Matt. 13:58). Unbelief is one hindrance to the ideal of God.

There are fundamental facts of cause and effect, sowing and reaping, which hinder God's ideal. A man who has openly violated the laws of hygiene and health is going to pay for it. Being saved from one's sins doesn't always abolish the penalty for long-standing neglect. God's ideal, then, is for wholeness of the person—not just wholeness of the body!

II. WHOLENESS IS GOD'S GIFT

Divine healing is not a divine right! We cannot demand it from God. Healing is a gift from the hand of God—something needed, but not deserved.

Divine healing was given in a time of expectancy. Luke wrote: "The apostles performed many miraculous signs and wonders among the people. And all the believers used to meet together in Solomon's Colonnade" (Acts 5:12).

On the Day of Pentecost 3,000 people were saved. After the healing of the lame beggar the Christians had multiplied until there were 5,000 households. Probably at the point of Acts 5:12-16 the followers of Jesus numbered more than 10,000. Since the group was too large to meet in an upper room or any available halls, the Christians gathered in the Temple precincts at the place known as Solomon's Porch or Colonnade. According to tradition, it was a section still standing from Solomon's original Temple. That portico, facing the east, caught the early morning sunlight and was thus a favorite meeting place in the morning hours.

An aura of excitement and expectancy pervaded the atmosphere as these joyful new Christians met to hear about Jesus and to praise God in the power of the Spirit.

William Barclay pointed out that Acts 5:12 tells us certain things about the Church:

> (i) It tells us where the Church met . . . These early Christians were constant in their attendance at the House of God. Daily they kept their appointment with God. They desired ever to know God better and ever to draw upon God's strength for life and living. And where could they be nearer God than in God's House?
> (ii) It tells us how the Church met. The early Christians assembled in the place, where, of all places, everyone could see them. They had no idea of hiding their Christianity . . . They were determined to show all men whose they were and where they stood.
> (iii) It tells us that the Early Church was a supremely effective Church. Things happened . . . Men will always throng to a Church wherein men's lives are changed.[3]

Divine healing was given in a time of honesty. Luke adds: "No one else dared join them, even though they were highly regarded by the people. Nevertheless, more and more men and women believed in the Lord and were added to their number" (Acts 5:13-14). Since God's judgment against insincerity put Ananias and his wife into the grave, people in and out of the Church went through a period of self-examination.

Honesty before God allows Him to purify and cleanse His Church. The pure Church is a powerful Church—one in which God's healing takes place. Such honesty before God and the Church would avoid basic errors that many popular faith healers commit.

One error is the refusal to recognize God at work through medical science as well as in spiritual healing. All healing comes from God's hand. Dr. Ephraim McDowell, a Kentucky surgeon, always prayed before surgery: *Direct me, O God, in performing this operation, for I am but an instrument in Thy hands.*

A second error is the unreasonable claims made for miraculous healing without trained diagnosis or knowledge of the facts.

A third error is the excessive publicity of healing services. Human misery is exploited to get an audience under the lights and television cameras. How unlike Jesus who consistently commanded, "Don't tell anybody about it. Go home and say nothing more!" Jesus didn't want physical healing to become a top priority over His ministry of spiritual healing.

A fourth error is the assumption that when symptoms cease, the problem has been cured. The final test is the fact of wholeness.

A fifth error committed by faith healers is the cruelty of suggesting that the failure to get well is due to one's own lack of faith. It is a face-saving device by the "faith healer." Many sick persons are driven deeper into depression by a vague sense of guilt when told their lack of faith is the cause of no results.

Divine healing takes place best when people are being honest before God. That kind of openness with God allows wholeness to happen!

Leslie D. Weatherhead told of a young girl who went to the Lourdes shrine in France in search of healing. She was given a silver cross which had been blessed by a priest. She was instructed to hold the cross tightly when the Host was elevated—and she would be healed! She did her best, but to no avail.

Finally, she went home to England to die. "As she lay dying," said Dr. Weatherhead, "she gave the cross to me and said, 'I want you to keep it, for it taught me a great lesson. I have learned not to hold the cross and believe that I shall be healed, but to yield myself utterly to the Crucified One and not mind whether I am healed or not.'"

Divine healing was given in a time of seeking. Luke recorded: "As a result, people brought the sick into the streets and laid them on beds and mats so that at least Peter's shadow might fall on some of them as he passed by. Crowds gathered also from the towns around Jerusalem, bringing their sick and those tormented by evil spirits, and all of them were healed" (Acts 5:15-16).

Since crippled, sick, and deformed people weren't welcome inside the Temple precincts by the rulers, the Christians went out to them in the streets. The weak and feeble had been brought by friends to seek the help of the Church. Interestingly, people expected the Church to be able to offer healing from the Lord. Divine healing comes to those who are seeking God's gift of wholeness.

One woman had a tumor and sought prayer for God's healing. The next morning the tumor had disappeared. Though scheduled for surgery, she had been healed by direct intervention.

Another woman faced a similar operation. She, too, sought for God's help. She had been apprehensive and fearful. After prayer for God's divine intervention, however, she went to surgery unafraid and peaceful. A rapid recovery followed the operation and she suffered virtually no pain or anguish.

Both ladies sought God's help—and got it. The avenue

of healing differed, but God gave wholeness to each! Wholeness is God's gift.

III. WHOLENESS IS GOD'S DOING

Sometimes Jesus healed directly with a spoken word. At other times, He touched the sick. On still other occasions, the Master used material media—the hem of His garment, the clay applied over blind eyes, and oil to anoint the sick. Sometimes His healings were instantaneous, and at other times, gradual. However God chooses to bring healing, wholeness is still God's doing.

In Acts 5:12-16, people sought to get in Peter's shadow—but any healing was not Peter's doing, but God's. Peter was simply being himself, going about his duties, forgetting himself. His unconscious influence was mightier than what he had done deliberately up to that time. And we all cast shadows of influence by what we say, by what we do, and by what we are. The restoration of wholeness was God's doing and is still today.

Some may ask, "Is there such a thing as divine healing?"

It must be asked, "Is there any other kind?" All healing is from God's hand.

God gave physical healing. The sick were brought and physical healing happened! Time and space does not permit the tracing of many instances of physical healing even in our days.

One example is the story of Jimmy Richey, a member of Decatur, Ala., First Church of the Nazarene. On October 15, 1962, he became paralyzed after three major operations and two minor surgeries as well as a battery of tests involving 35 doctors. That year, Mr. Richey spent 179 days in the hospital, according to a report in the *Herald of Holiness* magazine. For 14 years Jimmy Richey could not walk, and he became very lonely and depressed.

However, on June 2, 1976, while watching a religious telecast, he felt impressed: "Today is my day for healing." As a woman sang "Rise and Be Healed" on the program, he sensed God's touch and stood to his feet. With tears of joy flowing down his cheeks, Jimmy Richey took his first steps—and he has been walking ever since. From his own personal testimony, many people have become Christians, some have been healed, and others filled with the Holy Spirit.

God gave emotional healing. Luke noted, "Crowds gathered . . . bringing their sick and those tormented by evil spirits" (Acts 5:16). Those with troubled minds came to Jesus. The verb "tormented" comes from a noun which means "crowd," or "to be in a tumult." People's emotions can become so frayed by the pressures of life, it's like being hassled in a huge crowd, a state of tumult! When one can't stand the crashing of snowflakes as they hit the ground, he has had enough!

Man is not only body. The state of his mind and emotions can make him sick and debilitated. If he is tense with nerves, or bitter with resentments, or if he has a sense of dull hopelessness—then he can't do much for himself. But God can! God can give emotional healing.

Sometimes—in fact, most times—the emotional sicknesses and scars are more serious and deadly than the physical ailments.

A boy was born with a shriveled right leg. From infancy he had to wear a brace on his leg. As he got older, he realized he couldn't compete with his useless leg. Unable to play games, climb trees, or run like other boys, he got the impression he could not climb the ladder of life. A deep sense of limitation and inferiority settled over his whole outlook on life. It went into his mind and emotions as he brooded over the handicap.

One day his father told him about a great cathedral

where there was a pile of crutches and braces left by people who had gone there and been healed. He added, "Someday I'm going to take you there, when I think you have matured enough so that you can believe. Then we will pray and ask the Lord to heal you so you can leave your brace on the altar."

Finally the great day came. Dressed up in their best, father and son entered the cathedral. Sunlight came streaming through the beautiful stained-glass windows. The great pipe organ reverberated through the sanctuary. As they approached the altar, his father said, "Son, kneel and pray. Ask the Lord to heal you."

The lad prayed earnestly with faith asking God to heal him. He turned and looked at his father. Though he had seen him in many different situations before, he said later, "I will always remember the beauty on my father's face at that moment. There were tears in his eyes, and shining through was the joyous faith of the true believer."

The boy was stirred deeply—and stood up. Looking down, there was his withered leg—just as before. Depressed and despondent, the boy started down the aisle with his father, the old brace thumping along as usual. As they came to the door of the cathedral, something happened! In the boy's words:

"I felt something tremendously warm in my heart. I seemed to feel something like a great hand pass across my head. Suddenly I was boundlessly happy. I cried, 'Father, you are right! I have been healed! I have been healed!'

"Young as I was, I knew what had happened. God had not taken the brace off my leg, but He had taken the brace off my mind."

From that moment on, the boy was never dismayed about his withered leg. In fact, he grew in faith and confidence and developed until he became a newspaper editor. It was more important for him to have God's healing for his emotions than it was to have just a physical healing. Wholeness is God's doing!

God gave spiritual healing. Amid the excitement, it was more than sensationalism. Luke says, "More and more men and women believed in the Lord and were added to their number" (Acts 5:14). Many were having God's touch of healing on their souls—forgiving sins, removing guilt, adding the new life in Christ. The Greek imperfect tense infers that new Christians were being added continuously or repeatedly. It was a spiritual healing which was taking place more than any other kind. Spiritual restoration is God's ministry of wholeness.

God wants to heal the hurts in man's spirit. Those who were only healed physically eventually died. But those who were healed in their souls were made whole for eternity! The deepest need is spiritual healing.

A woman in Indiana wrote a letter describing her spiritual healing:

> Eight years ago my life was in a negative state—and that is putting it mildly. Knowing that something must be done, I finally decided to dust off the Bible and have a regular hour for prayer and meditation.
>
> For two solid years I studied, meditated, prayed, disciplined myself—but nothing happened.
>
> Then one night, very late, everyone in bed, when I was at a point where I felt I had done just about everything to improve situations, I knelt down and cried out everything to God. This wonderful peace crept over me. I knew God cared for me. I just felt it. As I later understood, I had reached a complete relinquishment after a period of repentance and godly sorrow.
>
> This experience changed my whole life. It was so wonderful that when I tell about it I sometimes forget to mention the physical healing that took place—so much more important to me was the healing of my soul. Three physical ailments were wiped out.
>
> The next day I began a cleanup of my whole life, making restitution wherever I could. Now I actually feel

joy in the midst of perplexing situations. And I have a courage that amazes me. Fear is gone and I am sure there is a beyond, a very beautiful one. God enables me to experience a rebirth or awakening of the soul that keeps growing and growing. My! How exciting life is![4]

Luke closed on this note: "and all of them were healed" (Acts 5:16). God has healing for His children. Wholeness is God's ideal; wholeness is God's gift; wholeness is God's doing. Whatever one's illness—physical, emotional, spiritual —he should begin with God's touch of wholeness. As he comes to God in prayer, he must let God do His work in him in His way and in His time!

The Bible teaches: "Is any one of you sick? He should call the elders of the church to pray over him and anoint him with oil in the name of the Lord. And the prayer offered in faith will make the sick person well; the Lord will raise him up. If he has sinned, he will be forgiven. Therefore confess your sins to each other and pray for each other so that you may be healed. The prayer of a righteous man is powerful and effective" (Jas. 5:14-16).

The suffering person is encouraged to seek God's healing touch of wholeness. We have a great Savior, the Great Physician. God will either heal or give something better!

3

Square Pegs
in Round Holes

Acts 5:17-42

Winston Churchill described Russia as "a riddle wrapped in a mystery inside an enigma."[1]

Ever since the Day of Pentecost when the Holy Spirit fell upon the waiting disciples, the secular world has looked upon the born-again Christian in the same way: "a riddle wrapped in a mystery inside an enigma." The genuine born-again Christian in this old world is forever a square peg in a round hole! He just doesn't fit! He belongs to another kingdom and marches to a different drumbeat. People will never understand why the real Christian cannot conform to discarded values.

For centuries Christians have had to learn to deal with rejection. The forms of rejection are many—but are always near the surface in one's relationships to an ungodly world: condescending tolerance, ridicule, utter indifference, open opposition, and even persecution.

As crowds gathered in Jerusalem to rejoice in the enthusiasm and excitement of the Early Church, the high priest and his fellow Sadducees were "filled with jealousy" (Acts 5:17). Luke described them with a word *(zelou)* which originally meant "to· boil" *(zeo)*. The Sadducees couldn't tolerate the Spirit-filled Christians, and it made them boiling mad!

Already Christians were square pegs in round holes! They just did not fit into the old molds of their society. Sadducees believed only in the present world. The idea of life after death, of judgment and heaven, of the resurrection was outside their rationalistic beliefs.

On the other hand, the Pharisees were legalists and ritualists. They prescribed external actions as if God were a scorekeeper of rights and wrongs. Spirit-filled Christians just don't fit either way! They never will!

The Sadducees were so angry they put the apostles into the Temple jail overnight and called for a meeting of the entire Sanhedrin to pass judgment the next morning. During the night, however, God sent an angel who secretly released the apostles from jail and commanded them: "Go, stand in the temple courts . . . and tell the people the full message of this new life" (Acts 5:20).

When the Sanhedrin met the next morning and began proceedings against the apostles, the high priest called for the prisoners to be brought before them. Of course, the cell was empty, even though the doors were locked! What a surprise! Imagine the embarrassment of the high priest! As thoughts were racing through his mind, another messenger arrived: "Look! The men you put in jail are standing in the temple courts teaching the people" (v. 25). There's a note of comedy in all the confusion!

Temple guards were sent out to bring the apostles into court—but with instructions to be cautious! Up to this point, opposition had only taken the form of warnings and threats. However, this event sets overt persecution into motion; and Spirit-filled Christians have never fit since—square pegs in round holes!

A man said to Dwight L. Moody long ago: "Now that I am a born-again Christian, do I have to give up the world?"

Mr. Moody replied: "No, you don't have to give up the world. If you give a good, ringing testimony for the Son of God, the world will give you up real quick! They won't want you around!"

If one is determined to be Christlike, he will not fit any more than Jesus did. In fact, Jesus prayed on the eve of His crucifixion for all of His people: "I have given them your word and the world has hated them, for they are not of the world any more than I am of the world. My prayer is not that you take them out of the world but that you protect them from the evil one. They are not of the world, even as I am not of it" (John 17:14-16).

Acts 5:17-42 gives a good lesson on what to do when one doesn't fit. If one has already discovered that total surrender to Christ makes him feel like a square peg in a round hole, this passage of scripture gives a note of encouragement.

I. Even Though One Doesn't Fit, He Can Expect God's Deliverance

The apostles locked in jail got inside help—it was God's doing. "An angel of the Lord opened the doors of the jail and brought them out" (Acts 5:19). It is almost comical that God sent an angel to release "the apostles from the custody of the Sadducees who didn't believe in angels!"[2]

One can expect God to deliver His people because the whole Bible is the story of one escape after another: Noah's deliverance from the Flood, Israel's deliverance from Egyptian slavery, the believer's deliverance from sin.

God has purposes in man's deliverance. A careful look at Acts 5 reveals that God didn't save the apostles from a head-on collision with the Sanhedrin.

The apostles were delivered from jail for a sign. It was a sign to the apostles that God was still in charge. He had not abandoned them. Therefore, the men could have even greater confidence in God's care.

It was also a sign to the unbelieving Jews that they were opposing God's men. It was a warning from God who was still trying to reach His chosen people. While the Sadducees had given up on God, He had not given up on them. They who did not believe in God's intervention were given a sign that God can and does intervene in the affairs of men! God's deliverance is a sign that He is behind the scenes, working all things together for good for those who love Him.

Arnold Airhart pointed out: "The Lord will not crush their opposition so that it ceases altogether. Yet there is assurance that He is always able to take care of any situation concerning them. They will not be immune to trials and setbacks; yet He will know where they are and what they are enduring at any time."[3]

The apostles were delivered from jail for service. They were set free so they could continue their ministry, not retreat into safety. It is noted: "God never releases a man from a tight spot for that man to have an easy time of it: He has bigger plans in mind for that person. . . . There was a purpose behind that deliverance: to have them go right back to the temple and continue their testimony for the Risen Jesus Christ."[4]

Two Nazarene missionaries, Armand Doll and Hugh Friberg, were imprisoned in Moçambique in 1975. Around the world, Nazarenes united in prayer and the United States government carried on arbitration. At last, these two men were set free.

After a furlough, each of them has been reassigned and are serving today as missionaries. Deliverance came as a step toward continued service and ministry.

One can expect God to deliver from opposition and pressing circumstances for a reason: greater service for Jesus Christ!

God has lessons in deliverance. He wants His people to learn some things from their times of pressure and persecution.

First, one should ask God to deliver him in God's own time and in His own way.

Second, one should expect God to deliver him sometime and somehow. Who can guess how God will do it? These apostles probably never dreamed that God would deliver in the way He did. One must hang on to this thought: "God has a master key that will unlock all the prison doors where His servants may be incarcerated by the enemy. 'The Lord knoweth how to deliver the godly out of temptation' (II Pet. 2:9 KJV)."[5]

Third, one should wait for God to act. The disciple of Jesus must be patient and allow God to work things out in His own time. He must not pry open doors or eliminate people from his circle of friendships. There is danger in trying to move ahead of God's timing.

A group of tourists went down into Mammoth Cave in Kentucky. When they reached an area called "The Cathedral," the guide climbed up a rock designated "The Pulpit." He said he would preach a sermon—a short one! All he said was: "Keep close to your guide!"

The tourists could see that was good advice down in the dark caverns.

And it's good advice to the Christian who feels like a square peg in the round hole of an unsympathetic, misunderstanding world.

Fourth, one should recognize God's deliverance however it happens. Jesus' followers must not have preplanned methods of how God should do it. God does not always answer with an angel! One must learn to recognize God's hand behind the scenes. He doesn't work the same way every time.

In the courtyard of a Russian prison, a godly Christian

stood among a group of Russian criminals. He was chained like the others and sentenced to go to Siberia because he would not denounce Christ.

His fellow prisoners jeered at him: "But you're not better off than we are. You are wearing the handcuffs just like we are. If your God is of any use to you, why doesn't He knock off your chains and set you free?"

The faithful Christian replied reverently: "If the Lord will, He can set me free even now. And, though my hands are chained, my heart is free!"

The disciple must recognize real deliverance when it comes. One can expect God's deliverance!

II. EVEN THOUGH ONE DOESN'T FIT, HE CAN OBEY GOD'S COMMANDS

When brought before the council, the apostles were told by the high priest: "We gave you strict orders not to teach in this name . . . Yet you have filled Jerusalem with your teaching and are determined to make us guilty of this man's blood" (Acts 5:28). Could they have forgotten their words to Pilate at Jesus' trial? "Let his blood be on us and on our children!" (Matt. 27:25).

The apostles answered the high priest, "We must obey God rather than men!" (Acts 5:29). Even though they didn't fit, they obeyed God!

Obedience involves listening to what God has to say. The apostles had not been so occupied with their new freedom that they had failed to hear God's command: "Go, stand in the temple courts . . . and tell the people the full message of this new life" (v. 20).

While men had commanded, "Keep still," God commanded, "Speak out!" The apostles listened to God. They had to choose. God's men soon learned their message was more important than their safety and comfort! Some would have preferred to drop the testifying business. Others would have just as soon testified in some safe place. But God commanded them to go before the people in the Temple. And they went as He commanded.

Obedience involves doing what God wants done! Dr. Richard C. Halverson once said: "The Great Commission leaves no room for debate. Jesus Christ commanded His Church to carry the gospel into all the world. Her only alternative is to disobey!"

A king once ordered one of his subjects to do a very difficult thing. "But that's impossible," argued the subject.

"I didn't ask for your opinion," returned the king, "but for your obedience!" And God wants our obedience, not our opinions.

God wanted witnesses, not lawyers! Since that band of Christians was faithful to speak in the Temple, God was able to use them as witnesses to the leaders of the nation. Brought from the Temple to the courtroom, they testified: "The God of our fathers raised Jesus from the dead—whom you killed by hanging him on a tree. God exalted him to his own right hand as Prince and Savior that he might give repentance and forgiveness of sins to Israel. We are witnesses of these things" (Acts 5:30-32).

God wanted witnesses of a living Christ. Without faltering, Peter stood on the resurrection of Jesus as God's method of giving forgiveness of sins and eternal life to all who believe in Him. In fact, Peter used a very special word to describe Jesus (v. 31):

> The word in Greek is *archegos*, a seaman's term. In Peter's day, many ships had a crew member who was an unusually strong swimmer. If anything happened to the ship, this crewman would tie a rope around his waist, dive overboard and swim to shore. After attaching the rope on shore, he would assist others who were making their way to safety by clinging to the line. His name was the *archegos*.
>
> Peter thought of Jesus as The Archegos in life. Je-

sus, to Peter and the others, was the powerful life-saver who made possible the crossing from death to life![6]

In Jonathan Edwards' diary are these words: "Resolved, first, that every man ought to obey Christ without hesitation or reserve. Resolved, second, whether anybody else does or not, I will, so help me God!"

Obedience involves depending upon what God desires to give. Peter spoke of "the Holy Spirit, whom God has given to those who obey him" (Acts 5:32). The fellow who is honestly obeying God's directions will experience the wonder of the Holy Spirit. To those who would do God's will is given God's enablement. He never asks us to do a thing or to endure a thing without giving His Spirit to empower us. God gives himself to those who obey Him.

Queen Elizabeth once asked an English merchant to go on a mission representing the crown. He hesitated because he was afraid his long absence would be fatal to his business. The queen replied, "You take care of my business, and I will take care of yours!"

When he returned from the long journey representing the queen, he found his business, by the patronage of the queen, had increased in volume. He was richer than when he left.

In response to our obedience, God gives His Holy Spirit as a down payment of more to come. We can depend on Him.

III. Even Though One Doesn't Fit, He Can Rejoice in God's Approval

The witness of the apostles enraged the Sanhedrin to the point they wanted to kill them. Gamaliel asked for an executive session to calm things down. After the Christians were sent out, he made a plea of tolerance and patience, concluding: "For if their purpose or activity is of human

47

origin, it will fail. But if it is from God, you will not be able to stop these men, you will only find yourselves fighting against God" (Acts 5:38-39).

As a result of his speech, "They called the apostles in and had them flogged. Then they ordered them not to speak in the name of Jesus, and let them go" (v. 40). Thirty-nine times the lash broke into each man's flesh—it was a brutal punishment as well as public disgrace.

However, notice their reaction: "The apostles left the Sanhedrin, rejoicing because they had been counted worthy of suffering disgrace for the Name" (v. 41). They were proud to be associated with Jesus and honored to share in the fellowship of His sufferings.

Jesus had told them earlier: "Blessed are those who are persecuted because of righteousness, for theirs is the kingdom of heaven. Blessed are you when people insult you, persecute you and falsely say all kinds of evil against you because of me. Rejoice and be glad, because great is your reward in heaven" (Matt. 5:10-12).

James and John had not always reacted this way when they didn't fit. Back in a Samaritan village, the people had not welcomed them. They reacted by wanting to call down fire from heaven to destroy their tormentors. But now, after being threatened and beaten, they are rejoicing!

William McCumber noted in one of his editorials: "Between these two events was Pentecost, when the Holy Spirit filled and cleansed the hearts of Jesus' disciples. The change that took place in [James and John] has taken place in the lives of thousands of believers. The sanctifying power of the Spirit, and the abounding grace of God, can effect deep and continuing changes in our hearts and lives."

Born-again Christians may rejoice even though they don't fit. They are not after men's applause but God's approval.

John Huss preached against the evils of religious leaders in his day. He was excommunicated, brought before the Council of Constance, charged with treason, and sentenced to die as a heretic.

A paper hat was made for his head with the inscription: "A ringleader of heretics." John Huss replied: "My Lord Jesus Christ for my sake did wear a crown of thorns; why should not I then for His sake wear this light crown, be it ever so ignominious? I will wear it willingly!"

When the mock hat was put on his head, the presiding bishop chanted: "Now we commit thy soul unto the devil."

"But I," responded John Huss, looking toward the heavens, "do commend into Thy hands, O Lord Jesus Christ, my spirit which Thou hast redeemed."

As his executioners chained him to the stake to be burned, he smiled with love, saying: "My Lord Jesus Christ was bound with a harder chain than this for my sake, and why then should I be ashamed of this rusty one?"

On that day, July 6, 1415, he asserted, "What I taught with my lips I now seal with my blood." And, singing a hymn in a loud and cheerful voice, he was burned at the stake.

Our world will never understand these words: "Blessed is the man who perseveres under trial, because when he has stood the test, he will receive the [victor's] crown of life that God has promised to those who love him" (Jas. 1:12).

Someone put it eloquently:

> The quality of the disciples' lives made their testimony trustworthy. They were honest men. They taught men to live pure and holy lives. They were not trying to please the people, to be popular, to get a favorable hearing. They were good men who taught other men to be good. They were ready to risk everything for the privilege of preaching the truth. They lived holy, just and honorable lives. Their preaching had the note of sincerity. They were not frauds or imposters.

They rejoiced that they should be counted worthy to suffer shame and martyrdom for the sake of Jesus!

A commander was facing a great battle soon. He inspected his troops. Seeing a group of undisciplined, inexperienced men, he said to one of his generals: "These men I know nothing about."

As he passed another group, he recognized them. They had been trained under his officers for a short time. He knew they could march, bivouac, maneuver on the battlefield. To his general he commented: "These men I think I can trust."

Finally the commander came to a division of troops who had been with him through many campaigns. They were veterans of battle. They had been baptized in blood and fire in many fierce and deadly struggles. As the men stood stiffly before him, ready and waiting, the commander said with pride and confidence: "These men I know and trust!"

When one faces those testings and trials and inner sufferings because he just doesn't fit in an ungodly world, he may rejoice with Job: "When he has tested me, I will come forth as gold" (Job 23:10).

One's greatest danger is not opposition in any of its forms. That helps make him strong and pure. One's greatest danger is when all men speak well of him, when his firm convictions are patronized by an unbelieving world.

It is often through hardship and trial,
  And tragedy, patiently borne,
God's enabling strength is given,
  And beauty and joy are born.

Overcoming is joy in itself;
  And sorrow, through God's wondrous grace,
Etches deeper the strong lines of courage
  In the overcomer's face.

Back in the early days of World War II, Martin Niemoller was a pastor in Germany. The Nazi government told him to preach one thing; God told him to preach another. As a result, he spent eight years in Hitler's prison camps, including Dachau—quite a price for obeying God rather than man.

Niemoller preached on June 27, 1937, his last sermon before being arrested. Apparently Nazi spies were in the audience. His text was Acts 5:34-42 and his sermon was entitled "Here I Stand!"

Already many evangelical pastors had been arrested and convicted on trumped-up charges. The sifting process had already begun in the congregations: the real, born-again Christians remaining true; the halfhearted, nominal Christians slipping away. Here are his closing words:

> Then, my dear friends, what next? Joy and comfort? Or despair and intimidation?
> There is indeed no hope except to hold firmly to the Crucified One and learn to say in simple and certain faith, "In the bottom of my heart Thy Name and cross alone shine forth at all times and in all hours, and therefore I can be glad." It may be long until we are truly glad, until like the apostles we are counted worthy to suffer shame for Jesus' name. The way will not be opened today or tomorrow. And that may be good, for it may teach us not to take impressions for belief. It may teach us how, in the heat of the struggle, to mark the word of our Lord and to continue to hear the message of the cross, the gospel of Jesus Christ—perhaps for the first time aright. It may show us how to teach it and to hear it and to preach it; for our faith lives in this Word, and our joy flows from this Word.[7]

Our Heavenly Father doesn't promise an easy journey for His children. But He does guarantee a safe landing!

Square pegs in round holes! A real Christian just won't ever fit in this old world. Even though he doesn't fit, he can expect God's deliverance, obey God's commands, and rejoice in God's approval.

In our homes, in our places of work, in our classes at

school, even in our circles of friends and loved ones, are many pressures and tests which cause inner hurt. Rejection is never easy. Sometimes it hurts too much to talk about, to even admit to oneself. But we can pray about it. God is concerned.

Sometimes a child is so sick, it just cannot lie in bed any longer. The mother has to pick him up and hold him. And sometimes God's children are so troubled they cannot lie at rest anywhere but in God's lap while He bends over them and sings, "As a mother comforts her child, so will I comfort you" (Isa. 66:13).

An unknown hymn writer has caught the spirit of God's faithful promise:

The soul that on Jesus hath leaned for repose
I will not, I will not desert to his foes;
That soul, though all hell should endeavor to shake,
I'll never, no never, no never forsake.[8]

4

Geared to Go and Grow

Acts 6:1-7

A pastor once announced, "I've resigned my pastorate and have signed a contract to teach school this year so I can get something done for God."

He, like many pastors today, had become a jack-of-all-trades and master of none. Trained to preach, he found himself as an office manager, a detail man, an architect, an ex officio chairman of a multitude of committees.

The man admitted, "Sure, they let me preach on Sunday, but the real emphasis was usually on how I could organize, engineer, create publicity, and a multitude of other chores."

By teaching in the school, he would have more time after work for witnessing and winning people to Christ. It is a sad commentary on the church of today—but many, many pastors, at least secretly, share his feelings.

Something pathetic has happened in the contemporary church. Many people look on the pastor as a hired hand, a spiritual athlete, a religious superman! Meanwhile, hosts of good laymen are dying on the vine from atrophy. Not only do laymen think the pastor can do everything around the church, tragically, pastors begin to think it is true, also! And the gap between overworked pastors and underchallenged and underachieving laymen widens. Both clergy and laity must learn to distinguish between being busy and being productive.

At such frenetic paces, the pastor gets confused, wondering whether the people are following him or chasing him! Too many pastors are like the small boy trying to lead a large dog. A man watching asked, "Where are you taking that big dog?"

"Don't know yet," replied the boy. "But when he decides where he wants to go, I'll take him there!"

While the Bible takes the reader on flights of great faith and heavenly glory, it also gets right down to everyday business. In the midst of all the excitement and drama of the Early Church in the Book of Acts, Luke records the pragmatic lessons needed even today. Spirit-filled pastors must learn what the apostles learned long ago when pressed by increasing demands: "It would not be right for us to neglect the ministry of the word of God in order to wait on tables. . . . We will turn this responsibility over to them and will give our attention to prayer and the ministry of the word" (Acts 6:2-4).

Laymen were selected to handle the material matters of the growing Church. Did God approve such an organization? The answer is found in the words: "So the word of God spread. The number of disciples in Jerusalem increased rapidly, and a large number of priests became obedient to the faith" (v. 7).

In graphic form, Luke has penned the reasons for lay leadership, the requirements of lay leadership, and the results of lay leadership. By this necessary step of organization, the Early Church was geared to go and grow! These same lessons are vital for the expansion and development of the Church today!

I. Reasons for Lay Leadership

First—the demands of Church growth created the need for lay leadership. As the community of believers grew, new situations kept coming up. Where there's life, there's growth. Where there's growth, there are problems. As the Word of God had been preached, multitudes were being brought into the Church. The Church grew in numbers, which in turn produced more areas of need and concern.

The Bible records, "And in those days, when the number of the disciples was multiplied" (Acts 6:1, KJV). Luke uses a new arithmetic for the first time. Previously Luke mentions that people were "added" to the Church. But in Acts 6 growth was so rapid, Luke describes it as multiplication. Churches who go and grow will face problems. The peaceful, quiet, undisturbed church is fast becoming a corpse!

Robert E. Maner wrote an article entitled "Growing Pains." He pointed out:

> There is the pain of lost leadership. An influx of new people means that some of them will take leadership from those now in office. Even sanctified people have difficulty relinquishing the reins to others. . . . The pain of diminished prominence! The more people we have, the less prominent any one person becomes. . . . So the loving attention must be shared with these new people. . . . The pain of shared success! . . . Keeping everybody busy in a place where they are best suited will prove to be a big but very vital job. The pain of directional uncertainty! This will soon be felt when churches begin to really grow. Where are these new people taking our church? What will they come up with next? . . .
>
> Growth has its own built-in risk. . . . Trust in others is always at the risk of hurt and failure. But unless we plan to have a church which is a one-man operation, we must take that chance. . . . The pain of an empty purse! Growth will cost money. In fact, it will

cost a lot of money in more ways than most think. . . .
In equipment, supplies, utilities, literature, the demands
placed upon the church from within and without will
begin to increase. People will prove to be a costly
advantage. When we add to this the unexpected fact
that our income does not keep pace with our growth,
there will be times when we begin to wonder if we are
going to be able to pay the bills. The plain truth is that
not all new people will be tithers the day they arrive.
Some never will be. They must be taught about Christian
stewardship. During this interim there will be anxious
moments for pastor and church board. . . . The alternative is to remain a pigmy church and that is even more
painful.[1]

A *second* reason for lay leadership—the dynamics of
differing backgrounds call for lay leadership. Luke noted,
"The Grecian Jews among them complained against those of
the Aramaic-speaking community" (Acts 6:1). Quickly
social distinctions developed. Rapid growth does not occur
across cultural barriers, but by allowing each culture to
reach out to its own people for Jesus Christ. Upon becoming
a Christian, a believer does not lose his identity as an
individual with all of his own unique backgrounds and
associations. Christian brothers must learn to respect these
differences in each other.

A Chinese diplomat listened carefully to a speech at a
church conference. When asked for his reaction, he replied:
"It was very interesting, but not very encouraging. As I
gather from the speaker's remarks, God is a white man, an
American, and a Baptist. Unfortunately, it isn't so: God is
really a yellow man, a Chinese, and a Methodist!"

The Grecian Jews were citizens of the Mediterranean
world. Their ancestral roots were not in Palestine for many
centuries in the past. Most had never spoken Hebrew or
Aramaic, but grew up with Greek, the commercial language
of the Western world. Their culture, language, interests, and
values were much different than the Palestinian Jews who

were narrowly sectarian. Neither group could fully understand the other—though they had come from both groups to become Christians! Interestingly, the Grecian Jews, as New Testament history will demonstrate, became the most aggressive group while, even in Acts, Peter and the apostles gradually recede into the background of influence.

Today, beside cultural, sociological, and national differences, there are two major differences in expressing commitment to the church: those with a shared heritage and those with shared goals. There must be caution not to allow these differences to become divisive; those with shared heritage can be viewed by some as the conservators of tradition, and those with shared goals can be viewed as proponents of change!

According to Lyle Schaller, members of the church who have shared heritage or roots have certain characteristics:

> a better-than-average level of giving, many women over 50 who have been together in *this* church for over 30 years, a self-image of being a conservative and evangelical congregation, . . . strong adult Sunday School classes or other groups in which the members have a deep loyalty to that class, several three- or four-generation families, an expectation that the youth and young adults of today are the leaders of *this* congregation of tomorrow, an above-average resistance to change, a large number of very loyal older women, several adults under 65 who have "retired" from active leadership roles in the church, relatively few persons aged 20-40 not related by blood or marriage to other members, three or four vigorous and able women leaders in the 30-45 age range who are daughters of members, an emphasis in the outreach of the congregation on "what people ought to do" rather than on the self-identified needs of people, a strong but shrinking women's organization, and a statistical record filled with a series of numbers getting smaller with the passage of time.[2]

Those members with shared goals often have these characteristics:

easy assimilation of new members into the life and fellowship of the congregation, a broad and varied program, very few third-generation members, a strong emphasis on "results" and accountability, a record of some members leaving in protest, dependence on designated giving to supplement the regular level of giving to the unified budget, the highly visible presence of several members with a contagious enthusiasm for "what our church is doing in ministry," a shared style of leadership, clearly understood staff responsibilities, an above-average turnover in membership, very few leaders, if any, who refer to this as a "Sunday morning" church, and the median age of the members under 55 and usually under 50.[3]

Neither group should be considered "good" or "bad." These just happen to be the contexts from which people come to the church. The person from the "shared heritage" will never fully understand the fellow with the "shared goals" background and vice versa. But both can work together to build the kingdom of God. It calls for strong lay leadership—from both classes of members.

A *third* reason for lay leadership—the distribution of administrative concerns pleads for lay leadership. Back in the days of the Early Church, the synagogues sent officials every Friday morning to collect food and cash from the markets, shops, businesses, and homes. The collections were given to the poor who had no other source of help. Each person was given enough food for two meals a day for one week. This special fund was called the *Kuppah,* meaning "the basket." Members of local synagogues also collected money daily to assist people in the unexpected tragedies and emergencies which leave people destitute. This collection was known as "the tray."

Apparently the Early Church followed these compassionate ministries. However, this money matter became the source of the first contention within the Church. Someone noted: "It is remarkable that both the internal disorders—

the hypocrisy recorded in Acts 5 and the murmurings recorded in Acts 6—sprang from the open-handed charity exercised toward the poor. . . . One root of bitterness grew in the givers, and another in the receivers."[4]

The poor apostles were being run ragged trying to implement this great ministry of mercy—and then got criticized for it. It's impossible to please everybody! The apostles desperately needed help! The Twelve didn't have the time to manage "tables." While the "tables" may include the dining tables, it more often referred to the money changer's tables. William LaSor wrote: "The Greek word for 'bank' *(trapeza)* is derived from the word for 'table,' [meaning] 'to conduct the financial affairs.' "[5] Lay leaders were needed to handle the general financial affairs of the church community.

Lay leadership is not inferior to the pastoral role, but complementary to it. "The Church needs amongst its officials men who have all kinds of gifts. The main gift of the apostles, of men like Peter and John, lay in preaching and teaching and instructing the people. The main gift of the Seven lay in practical administration of the affairs of the Christian Church. And the Church needed both kinds of gifts. . . . The Church needs its craftsmen as well as those who have the gift of speech."[6]

A *fourth* reason for lay leadership—the disciplines of prayer and preaching for pastors demand lay leadership. A pastor is called into the ministry by God's choosing. He is given two great gospel ordinances—prayer and preaching the Word. The pastor must be God's spokesman to the people through preaching the Word. And the pastor must be his people's spokesman to God through intercessory prayer! These are the two "musts" of his calling. However, under the pressures of administration, appointments, and a myriad of other important things, his time for prayer and study in the Bible are often the first to suffer. As a direct result, the spiritual climate and life of the people suffers—from spiritual malnutrition!

That's what the Twelve discovered as a grave danger, running here and there trying to distribute the financial affairs of the Church. They therefore delegated these chores so they might keep first things first: prayer and the Word. Those men who could not be drawn away from preaching in the name of Jesus by threats or beatings could neither be drawn away from preaching by money matters!

Some folk have wrongly interpreted such an attitude as a refusal to do "menial chores." However, it takes less discipline and gumption to do church business and church buildings than it does to shut oneself away from the action and activities and excitement in order to pray and prepare adequately for 20th-century congregations! Any pastor who has had firsthand experience at both knows it is a whole lot easier to build church structures than to fill them. Strong churches are not built around weak pulpits!

What the apostles discovered, every minister sooner or later learns—he cannot do everything well! Lay leadership is the Holy Spirit's answer to making the church go and grow.

II. REQUIREMENTS FOR LAY LEADERSHIP

After explaining the reasons for lay leadership, the Twelve said: "Brothers, choose seven men from among you who are known to be full of the Spirit and wisdom" (Acts 6:3). Incidentally, this is the first time "brothers" is used in the New Testament to describe Christians as spiritual brothers. It is used 34 times in Acts as well as in many references in the letters of the New Testament.

Here is the first step of internal organization within the Church. The selection of a church board is a very important and critical matter. It is much more significant than many church members have often realized.

Leonard Spangenberg, a layman from the eastern seaboard of the United States, once wrote a "Recipe for a Typical Church Board":

"Take one or two old-timers, add a son or daughter, tag on a 'know-it-all,' salt down with a maiden lady, stir up with a one-track-minded grammar school graduate, then put them all in a small room, and you have a fairly good sample of a church board."

However, the apostles set forth some high moral, spiritual, and intellectual qualifications for lay leaders.

The *first* requirement of lay leadership was to select men who were willing to serve. Generally, men willing to minister are more sensitive to other people's needs. Decision makers need to be also intuitive from the heart.

The Church was not choosing religious professionals, but laymen who, in reality, hold the power of influence within the church. The whole Church was to choose the lay leaders. Acts 6 is the introduction of the New Testament ideal of church government—a representative form, a republic. True democracy, in which every person participates in every decision, is not an ideal because most people are not qualified to handle all the problems in every aspect of the church's affairs. Historically, churches which have tried to adhere to strict democratic forms have often been marred by chaos and division. Thus, the selection of seven men was not an elevation to an elite class, but to a position of service. Leaders in God's kingdom are servers!

The *second* requirement of lay leadership was to select men who identified with the congregation. "Choose seven men *from among you*" (Acts 6:3). A lay leader must know the people whom he represents. Then, as now, he cannot remain aloof from the people or be absent often from the church's meetings and fellowship. A lay leader must identify with the community of faith.

The *third* requirement of lay leadership was the selection of men who were good witnesses. "Look ye out among you seven men of honest report" (v. 3, KJV). The word "report" has the same root as the Greek word for "witness" or "martyr." It means "good witnesses." The lay leader is to be a man well reported by others, but also the kind of man who would create a good report. In other words, he must have a good reputation as well as a good character. Reputation is what people think one to be. Character is what God and he know him to be.

Men chosen for leadership must be free from scandal. They must be trustworthy and known for their integrity. How many times the church has been marred by a leader who has gotten himself into compromising and embarrassing situations!

The Bible says, "A good name is more desirable than great riches" (Prov. 22:1). Jesus said it best: "Let your light shine before men, that they may see your good deeds and praise your Father in heaven" (Matt. 5:16).

The *fourth* requirement of lay leadership was the selection of men possessed and controlled by the Holy Spirit. The man full of the Spirit is not some weird ascetic who looks like he was chiseled out of frozen vinegar. He is a man living a normal Christian life—with a sense of laughter, a sense of fitness of things, a sense of God's divine leadings within. Holiness is wholeness! The sanctified man, filled with the Spirit of God, is one of God's most normal men, untwisted by dominating sin, unmarred by the self-despisings of guilt. He is a person as God intends him to be! As Stedman put it: "Spirituality is dependence on the activity of God, a recognition that God is within you and that He intends to work through you, and that you expect Him to do it."[7]

Stuart Briscoe commented:

When they were looking for seven businessmen to be responsible for church administration they insisted first of all that anyone who was not filled with the Holy Ghost need not apply. In those days suitability for administrative posts in the church was determined by spiritual condition! . . . How can we possibly hope to make an impact on our day and age when we neglect the basic considerations of God's requirements? . . . The men we elect to run the affairs of our churches are chosen for their business ability more than their spiritual integrity. By all means let us have businessmen for business positions in the church and give us educated men for educated congregations, but don't let us mistake ability that is natural, for dynamic that is spiritual. Filled with the Holy Spirit first, highly qualified second—that is the correct order.[8]

When the Holy Spirit "sees men elected to positions of leadership who lack spiritual fitness to cooperate with Him, He quietly withdraws and leaves them to implement their own policy according to their own standards, but without His aid."[9]

To elect men who are not filled with the Holy Spirit is to oust the Spirit from His place of leadership in the Church. Grieved and quenched, the Spirit departs, leaving carnal men to their own plans and power!

How can a congregation know if a man is filled with the Spirit? If he is filled with the Holy Spirit, there will be the fruit of the Spirit in his life! "The fruit of the Spirit is love" and that fruit of love is evidenced by "joy, peace, patience, kindness, goodness, faithfulness, gentleness and self-control. . . . Those who belong to Christ Jesus have crucified the sinful nature with its passions and desires. Since we live by the Spirit, let us keep in step with the Spirit" (Gal. 5:22-25).

The *fifth* requirement of lay leadership was to select men with good judgment and common sense. "Wisdom" means "practical wisdom." It is the ability to apply biblical knowledge to everyday life situations. The very first men appointed to church offices were not called to be great speakers, but were chosen for practical service! These lay leaders would need to have a sanctified common sense. Such a leader can see three things: what ought to be done, what can be done, and how to do it.

In 1 Timothy and Titus, Paul instructs leaders to be men who have shown wisdom in running their own home. If a fellow can't run his own affairs successfully and with wisdom, he is not a candidate for lay leadership. He will need all the wisdom God can give.

The church must look around and find men with these qualifications and elect them as lay leaders. God will only bless His Church as it operates by His standards and His requirements—not men's! Cattell observed, "But if men of proper spiritual qualifications are not at hand we will do well to ask ourselves why. Perhaps the reason is that we have for so long failed to give spiritual leadership, having been so fully occupied with serving tables, that now, looking about us, we cannot find 'seven men of honest report, full of the Holy Ghost and wisdom, whom we may appoint over this business.' "[10]

III. Results of Lay Leadership

The whole Church agreed that the election of seven lay leaders was the right thing to do. Having chosen seven, the candidates were brought to the apostles, who laid hands on them as a sign of God's blessing upon their service. Immediately some good results began to happen from this new organizational arrangement.

The *first* result—"The word of God spread" (Acts 6:7). The Word of God made an impact in two different ways.

First, the Word of God was spread by adequate and anointed preaching. Freed from the entangling details of the financial affairs, the apostles were able to give attention to their message of Jesus Christ. That precious time alone in prayer and preparation paid off in great dividends. Sticking closer to their preaching ministry, the Good News went further and had a greater impact. The fresh anointing of the Spirit only comes as a man is saturated in prayer and the study of God's Word.

Robert Hume, the Scottish philosopher and skeptic, walked many miles to hear John Brown of Haddington preach. Someone asked him why he went to such trouble to hear John Brown. He replied, "I go to hear him because he always preaches as though Jesus Christ is at his elbow!"

That kind of preaching isn't done by spontaneously flinging leftover biblical scraps. It only occurs as a man lives in the Word of God day after day, allowing the Spirit to guide and interpret its meaning for our day.

Second, the Word of God was spread by trained lay witnessing. The serious attention given to good preaching provided the content for training laymen in the life and ministry of Jesus. Through clear preaching, laymen were able to take hold of spiritual truth as weapons for evangelism. Someone pointed out, "The church is home *base* for evangelism, not necessarily the home *place* for evangelism." As trained laymen went out from the gathering place into their own workaday world, the Word of God spread in greater and greater concentric circles. It made an unforgettable impact on their world.

Stephen and Philip, among those chosen seven, became aggressive laymen in spreading the good news of Jesus Christ. Both men went out sharing the Scriptures.

Elton Trueblood admonished, "If you want a vital church constituency, make all within your society members of the crew and permit no passengers." After all, "The church is not a museum for the exhibition of eminent saints, but a workshop for the production of useful Christians!"

The *second* result—"The number of disciples in Jerusalem increased rapidly" (Acts 6:7). By the help of lay leader-

65

ship, more and more people came into contact with the good news of Jesus. God was upon them all as they labored interdependent upon one another within the Body of Christ. The Spirit of the Lord was so evident that many people repented, turned to God, and trusted in Jesus as Lord.

These new Christians weren't just converts, but became disciples—learners of Jesus! They had a yearn to learn—a good indication of a genuine conversion. Such a climate of faith is contagious! George Sweazy has remarked, "The most healthy possible atmosphere for a new Christian is found in a warmly evangelistic church which is so enthusiastic about its faith that it is eager to share it."

The *third* immediate result—"And a large number of priests became obedient to the faith" (Acts 6:7). Up to this point, prominent people had rarely become a part of the Christian movement. People, frozen out of the mainstream of Judaism by their sins or nonconformity, had gravitated to Jesus the Nazarene.

However, the priests who had periodically handled the dead sheep in the animal sacrifices, who had gone through the bloody rituals of the Temple, suddenly were confronted with reality. Indeed, Jesus was the fulfillment of all those types and signs and symbols. Dead sacrifices could never again touch the heart of one who had met the living Christ! Like a lover who had read and reread those special love letters, suddenly in the presence of his beloved, there is the spontaneous embrace—so it was that multitudes of priests awakened by the Spirit of God quickly embraced the Christ of the Cross and empty tomb. Those faithful men and their families found a sense of fulfillment in Jesus.

It cost them something to go with Jesus. They would feel the direct blows of hatred against the Christians. They would lose their status and livelihood as well as their friends. But to them, Jesus was real and they could never settle for less!

When pastors and Spirit-filled lay leaders work together as God directs, the impossible is bound to happen.

The late Fletcher Spruce once wrote:

> Let's face it! The church is a giant—a sleeping giant! The laity is largely asleep in the grandstands and the clergy is largely drugged—overwhelmed on the field of action. Our approach is the reverse of the New Testament pattern. We have seated the players in the grandstands and have sent the coach out on the field of action to face the enemy—almost singlehanded. Could this be a prime factor in the unbelievable inertia that plagues so many congregations today?[11]

The Church started as a lay movement. It was organized for lay leadership. Its pages of greatest history of going and growing were the eras of powerful lay involvement and lay movements. The local church should take seriously the selections of its lay leadership by seeking the guidance of the Holy Spirit. If we meet His requirements, we will get His results!

5

Trademarks of Holiness

Acts 6:8—8:1

The brief but vivid sketch of Stephen is echoed in a comment about a certain faithful pastor: "We are not nearly so grieved that he died as we are grateful that he lived!"

One of the seven lay leaders selected by the Early Church, Stephen handled the benevolent funds for people in special need. His duties became a springboard into an even greater Christian witness. As a result, Stephen became the first Christian martyr—sealing his witness with his own blood.

With the kingdom of God advancing by the multiplication of new believers, Satan couldn't tolerate the invasion. He began to fan the flame of jealousy and hatred among the Jews, particularly Jews from Africa and the provinces of Asia and Cilicia. Cilicia! The home province of Saul of Tarsus, a young, zealous, and brilliant debater against the Christian faith!

Unable to refute Stephen's witness and wisdom, the opposition resorted to bribery in order to gain false witnesses against Stephen: "We have heard Stephen speak words of blasphemy against Moses and against God" (Acts 6:11). Creating such a commotion, the Jews grabbed Stephen and arraigned him on trumped-up charges before the national council, the Sanhedrin. It was the same somber group which condemned and executed Jesus whom Stephen served!

Under the pressure of his last moments, Stephen's spirit was sweet and full of hope. That's the test of what's down inside! Problems don't make us good or bad, but simply reveal what we really are.

Outside a building in Russia hung a huge sign: "Committee on the Electrification of All Russia." However, at the door was another sign tacked up: "Bell out of order. Knock!"

Dr. E. Stanley Jones commented: "All our big signs . . . are canceled out if the thing doesn't work as power day by day—if the electricity doesn't make our doorbells ring. If our faith doesn't make us sing amidst sorrow and laugh at daily obstacles, then it lets us down. The Holy Spirit is religion as power—power available within."[1]

Reacting with animosity to Stephen's message, the Jews began grinding their teeth at him. Luke noted: "But Stephen, full of the Holy Spirit, looked up to heaven and saw the glory of God" (Acts 7:55). Being filled with the Spirit made all the difference in the world in Stephen's reaction under pressure. The Bible uses the word "sanctify" to describe the filling of a man's heart by the Holy Spirit. It is that gracious moment, in response to a man's faith, when the Holy Spirit takes full control, cleansing the heart by faith. The biblical word "holiness" describes the result of sanctification or cleansing. For example, sanctification is the cleaning up of the house, while holiness is the atmosphere after the house is clean.

The closing hours of Stephen's life reveal the "Trademarks of Holiness" in his heart. In Luke's account, there are at least five marks of holiness seen in Stephen. The inner serenity, guileless disposition, and Christlike bearing are evidences of Stephen's filling by the Holy Spirit. And more people are won to God by genuine holiness than by cleverness! The trademarks of holiness have significance in our day also.

I. A Radiant Character

Luke described it: "Now Stephen, a man full of God's grace and power" (Acts 6:8). "All who were sitting in the Sanhedrin looked intently at Stephen, and they saw that his face was like the face of an angel" (v. 15).

There was a winsomeness about Stephen as a result of being filled with the Holy Spirit. That hard-nosed abrasiveness, so typical of many religious people not at peace with themselves, is not consonant with the grace of an indwelling Christ. Holiness is a harmonizing experience between God and a man's nature.

The judges scrutinized Stephen for a clue of guilt or innocence on charges of blasphemy and treason. However, he seemed so at ease and open and trusting that he reminded them of an angel—one with nothing to hide, one simply and beautifully eager to do God's bidding.

When Moses came down from Mount Sinai, having been in the awesome presence of God, his face shone with the glory of God. Centuries later, Jesus, atop the Mount of Transfiguration, glowed with the purity of God's unique presence. And now Stephen, on the threshold of martyrdom, had the innocent glow with the glory of another world.

Yes, we do catch the light of the things we live with. "As 'the soul is dyed the color of its leisure hours,' so a man's environment is dyed the color of his inner life. If our inner life is a mass of merging shadows, those shadows are projected into the world around us until they finally hide the sun. If our inner life is illuminated by a light caught from the perpetual Light, that light is thrown upon the world we live in until even a cross is circled with glory."[2]

Character is what a person really is in his inner life. An old proverb says, "What is in the well will come up in the bucket." Henry Wadsworth Longfellow put it well:

> *Not in the clamor of the crowded street,*
> *Not in the shouts and plaudits of the throng,*
> *But in ourselves, are triumph and defeat.*

What those judges saw was not Stephen's performance but the outflow of his radiant character. His inner self had been made pure by the infilling of the Holy Spirit.

Pastor Jim Diehl told of a layman, George Comstock, praying: "O Lord, You know I am just like a sponge; and whatever I'm filled with, when I get squeezed, that's just what comes out. O Lord, so fill me with the Spirit of Jesus today that when I get squeezed this week, Jesus will come out."

In the pressure cooker, the Spirit of Christ oozed out of Stephen so much that his oppressors "saw that his face was like the face of an angel."

Paul wrote later, "And we, who with unveiled faces all reflect the Lord's glory, are being transformed into his likeness with ever-increasing glory, which comes from the Lord, who is the Spirit" (2 Cor. 3:18).

Roger Babson spent a day visiting with a close friend. The friend took him into a certain room in the house where there was an oil portrait of himself. Babson exclaimed: "That's a good picture! It looks exactly like you."

The host said, "Tell me the truth, please. Does it really look like me?"

Babson replied, "It's as fine a likeness as I have ever seen of anybody!"

"I have a notion to get down on my knees and pray," responded Babson's friend. He went on to explain:

One day the roof fell in on me financially. I was ready to destroy myself. A few days later an old friend, a portrait painter, invited me to lunch with him. I was so depressed I told him I would go some other time, if he would give me a rain check, because today I wasn't good company. But he insisted, and as we ate I was conscious of his close scrutiny. Finally, I asked him a bit irritably, why he was staring at me so. Slowly and quietly, he answered, "I would like to paint your portrait." I demurred, but when he insisted so strongly, I finally agreed. He wouldn't let me look at it until he had finished; then, before he took the cover off, he made a little speech. "I have painted what I see in you, not just your face, but your real self, your real heart and personality."

When I did look at it, I protested, "I'm not like that. That is not the face I see in the mirror." Many, many times I have stood here and prayed to my Heavenly Father to bring out the best that was in me. Today, you tell me it is a good likeness. Today, I realize redemption is not just for the soul; it is in part for here and now. I think of those words Jesus spoke to Simon Bar-jona, "Thou art Peter." Jesus changed him and me, too.[3]

That's the mark of a radiant character filled with the Holy Spirit.

II. An Effective Witness

Suddenly the defendant turned prosecutor! Acts 7 is Stephen's Bible-loaded witness before his judges. Though a lay leader, Stephen knew his Bible to the extent that he gave the first great survey of Israel's history and the progressive revelation of God. He saw the Old Testament in the light of Jesus' life, death, and resurrection. He found, as did Martin Luther: "The Old Testament is the cradle in which the Christ child is laid."

F. F. Bruce summed up Stephen's discourse with two main thoughts: "(1) God is not locally restricted and does not inhabit material buildings; His people similarly should not be tied to any particular spot; (2) the Jewish nation had always been rebellious; as previous generations opposed the prophets from Moses onwards, so this generation has killed 'the Righteous One.' "[4]

They who should have been conservators of God's Word were the very ones who had hindered God's work. Gradually the Jewish people had come to substitute rituals and rules and wealth in place of God's Word. They treated the Bible as if its presence were a magic wand or good luck charm.

A little boy noticed the unused Bible lying around his home. He finally asked his mother whose book it was. She replied, "It's God's Book."

The lad commented, "Well, we'd better give it back to Him. Nobody around here ever uses it."

Stuart Briscoe, disturbed by the complacency of Christians, noted:

> [Stephen] knew his Bible. . . . You will never speak with authority if you don't tell people what God says in language that they understand. And you will never be able to do this if you don't know your Bible. There is no short-cut to knowing the Word of God. There are no twentieth-century methods of instant Bible knowledge. We have instant coffee and instant potatoes, and, horror of horrors, instant tea! These are all devised to save time and energy, but there will never be an instant Bible-study method. You get your nose into the Book like Stephen—or you will never have anything irresistible to say.[5]

The holy heart has a hunger and thirst to know God's Word, and from that knowledge will flow an effective witness!

III. An Upward Look

Like any effective witness, Stephen's words comforted the afflicted and afflicted the comfortable. The crowd, having rejected Christ, became furious with anger, grinding their teeth like uncontrolled animals!

Luke swings the focus from the hostile mob to God's man of the hour: "But Stephen, full of the Holy Spirit, looked up to heaven and saw the glory of God, and Jesus standing at the right hand of God. 'Look,' he said, 'I see heaven open and the Son of Man standing at the right hand of God'" (Acts 7:55-56). The Greek text, translated "full of" or "being full" (KJV), does not portray a sudden moment of inspiration or infilling at this point of confrontation with his tormentors. "Being full" is descriptive of a permanent state or continuing relationship with God. Again, the pressure of the moment simply revealed the holiness of heart already existing in Stephen's life.

Instead of being influenced by the problems, of reacting with pessimism to the people surrounding him, Stephen got his bearings by the upward look! Men filled with fear would have only seen the tragic circumstances around him. But, Stephen, filled with the Holy Spirit, had no taste for that—he looked above his circumstances! The pure in heart look for the possibilities of faith. One writer added: "And then the heavens opened. He saw Jesus at the right hand of God. It was the reassurance that he needed. Love still reigned. Love still mattered. God still cared. Man still had a chance."[6]

Usually the Son of Man is portrayed in the Bible as sitting at the right hand of God. However, Stephen saw Jesus "standing at the right hand of God." Anyone who has ever been in the stadium when a baseball player just knocked in the winning run or when a football player has just made the winning touchdown can understand that. Everyone is on his feet, cheering and shouting with joy. And here, it is as if Jesus stood to cheer Stephen in his last lap, in his moment of triumph—the final victory! Jesus was identifying with Stephen, His faithful witness. Jesus was keeping

His promise, "Lo, I am with you alway, even unto the end of the world" (Matt. 28:20, KJV). The words of the Shepherd-King come echoing into our day: "Yea, though I walk through the valley of the shadow of death, I will fear no evil: for thou art with me" (Ps. 23:4, KJV).

In those last crucial moments, Stephen looked up—and saw Jesus standing to welcome him home and to place on his head the crown of life: "Be faithful, even to the point of death, and I will give you the crown of life" (Rev. 2:10).

The Spirit-filled man never settles for the grim view around him, but looks to Jesus, "the author and perfecter of our faith" (Heb. 12:2).

Turn your eyes upon Jesus;
Look full in His wonderful face;
And the things of earth will grow strangely dim
In the light of His glory and grace.[7]
—HELEN HOWARTH LEMMEL

IV. A COMMITTED TRUST

"At this they covered their ears and, yelling at the top of their voices, they all rushed at him, dragged him out of the city and began to stone him. Meanwhile, the witnesses laid their clothes at the feet of a young man named Saul.

"While they were stoning him, Stephen prayed, 'Lord Jesus, receive my spirit'" (Acts 7:57-59).

As Stephen saw Jesus rising and taking that first step toward him, Stephen responded by commending his spirit into the hands of Jesus! It was the evidence of a commitment to Jesus whom Stephen knew he could trust. Jesus is worthy of our trust!

Stephen's prayer of commitment, "Lord Jesus, receive my spirit," is certainly reminiscent of Jesus' prayer on the Cross: "Father, into your hands I commit my spirit" (Luke 23:46).

His was not a prayer for deliverance, but one of trust. There's no sound of fear in his voice—only faith. Stephen believed that whatever would happen, Jesus will be there and that Jesus is adequate for any emergency. While passing through the trial and coming death, Stephen simply prayed for Jesus to hold him steady, to keep him from failing.

At times, life is tough and things seem to go against us, but we can trust Christ to keep our spirit. He can keep us from fear, free from going sour and bitter, free from misplaced trusts.

Those angry men were successful in stoning Stephen, but they failed to stain him. Stephen's spirit was being kept out of reach by the sweet presence of Jesus Christ! The attitude of his prayer of trust reminds one of the statement by the missionary Judson: "I am not tired of my work, neither am I tired of the world. Yet, when Christ calls me home, I shall go with the gladness of a schoolboy bounding away from school!"

Harold Fickett wrote:

Lloyd C. Douglas in *The Robe* described Stephen slowly raising himself on his knees, holding one hand high and shouting triumphantly, "I see Him! My Lord Jesus—take me!" As he fell among the stones hurled at him, Marcellus turned from the scene and looked across at a soldier standing nearby. The soldier nervously commented that Stephen had thought he saw someone coming to rescue him. When Marcellus replied that Stephen really had seen someone coming, the soldier asked, "That dead Galilean, maybe?"

Marcellus replied, "That Galilean is not dead, my friend! He is more alive than any man here!"[8]

> *Trust Him when dark doubts assail thee;*
> *Trust Him when thy strength is small;*
> *Trust Him when to simply trust Him*
> *Seems the hardest thing of all.*

The Spirit-filled man doesn't have competing loyalties.

He instinctively commits his trust to Christ under pressure or not!

V. A Forgiving Spirit

A most remarkable thing occurred: "Then he [Stephen] fell on his knees and cried out, 'Lord, do not hold this sin against them'" (Acts 7:60). Kneeling in worship before the standing Christ, Stephen called out in prayer: "Lord, do not hold this sin against them!" No one can miss the similarity in spirit and in word between Stephen's prayer and that of Jesus on the Cross, "Father, forgive them, for they do not know what they are doing" (Luke 23:34). Yes, even in the squeeze of pressures and trials, the mind of Christ is revealed in the Spirit-filled man. It's "Christ in you, the hope of glory" (Col. 1:27).

Stephen's prayer showed his concern for the spiritual welfare of his tormentors, but it also underscored his belief in the forgiveness of God. The Lord is ready to forgive. Stephen could see the difference between the deed and the doer, the sin and the sinner. What's done is done, but the doer can be changed by God's great grace!

When George Wishart was to be executed, the executioner hesitated. Wishart stepped over to him and embraced him, saying: "Lo, here is a token that I forgive thee!"

A forgiving spirit flows from the Spirit-filled person as naturally as honey from the honeycomb. It's because the Spirit has cleansed the man's nature from that meanness and vindictive streak seen in carnal men. Alan Paton put it: "When a deep injury is done us, we never recover until we forgive!" A forgiving spirit is a trademark of holiness.

The lingering influence of a forgiving spirit is a powerful thing. Almost casually, Luke mentions a young antagonist guarding the coats of those stoning Stephen: "A young man named Saul" (Acts 7:58). The first sentence after describing Stephen's death, Luke adds, "And Saul was there, giving approval to his death" (8:1).

Stephen's sermon didn't impress Saul—but Saul could not escape the powerful, haunting influence of Stephen's forgiving spirit! Before long, that influence will erupt dramatically in Saul's heart. Indeed, God awakened life in Saul by the death of Stephen.

A college student listened only halfheartedly to a Memorial Day address which brought to his attention all the men who have sacrificed their lives fighting for freedom. Suddenly, he asked himself: "Am I worth dying for?"

That brought to his mind the awful waste of talent and personality which had been sacrificed in all of our country's wars. He felt that he, as a survivor, must make their sacrifices worthwhile. Those dead men spoke to him in a way no one else had. It changed his life's direction and purpose.

Some who are deaf to God's voice may be stirred by an echo of His voice in someone's example. The trademarks of holiness are evidences of spiritual reality in the Spirit-filled man or woman. The mark of a radiant character, the mark of an effective witness, the mark of an upward look, the mark of a committed trust, and the mark of a forgiving spirit are powerful and effective influences in a world out-of-sorts with itself.

One must remember: "Your life is influencing someone for good or for ill. Do not discount the bystander. He may be your silent partner. Stephen did not realize as he crumpled in death that the man who held the cloaks for those who threw the stones at him would actually become his own successor in the gospel and would carry it to limits of which he never dreamed."[9]

Elisabeth Elliot, widow of martyred missionary Jim Elliot, wrote: "To the casual observer, life ends in death. The truth is that death will end in life."

When Stephen died, he was ushered into the presence of Christ, the Giver of eternal life, but his influence was also being used to bring eternal life to young Saul—the apostle Paul in embryo form!

A pastor tried for several years to lead a skeptical young woman to Jesus Christ. It seemed she was cynical and indifferent to becoming a Christian. Before leaving to take another pastorate, he tried once more to present Christ to her, but seemingly without results. Finally he got up to leave. Suddenly she burst into tears, saying aloud: "I can believe on Jesus because I can believe in you. I do believe in Christ, because of your testimony and your life. You are real. Because of your sincerity, I can believe that your Jesus is real."

The trademarks of holiness in a godly, Spirit-filled life bore a harvest for Jesus Christ.

The only heaven some will ever see
Is the heaven they see in you and me!

6

Stamping the Fire—
Spreading the Sparks

Acts 8:1-8

When Stephen preached his famous sermon, one thing can be said for his audience: They certainly were not indifferent! In fact, his words struck right at their hearts—and triggered a period of persecution. With anger, the Jews took Stephen out and stoned him to death. The threat of arrest and imprisonment had hung in the atmosphere wherever Christians gathered, but everyone was stunned when Stephen was murdered.

Luke records: "On that day a great persecution broke out against the church at Jerusalem, and all except the apostles were scattered throughout Judea and Samaria. Godly men buried Stephen and mourned deeply for him. But Saul began to destroy the church. Going from house to house, he dragged off men and women and put them in prison" (Acts 8:1-3).

Young Saul of Tarsus was especially inflamed by Stephen's public witness. He hated everything Christian and immediately tried to stamp out this terrible "heresy." The King James Version translates it: "Saul . . . made havock of the church" (v. 3). The Greek verb "made havock" carried the idea of a "brutal and sadistic cruelty. It is used of a wild boar ravaging a vineyard into which he has broken, and of a wild animal savaging a body."[1] Inwardly torn by a "tortured conscience Saul tried through zealous activity to cover up his anxiety, emptiness, and hurt."[2] With all his energy, Saul attempted to extinguish the Church of Jesus Christ.

Harold L. Lundquist described it beautifully: "They tried to stamp out the fire of God in Jerusalem, but they scattered the embers all over the world!" As the flame of the Holy Spirit burned in the heart of the Early Church and began to cast a great light over the horizon, Satan must have determined: "This will never do. I'll stamp this out forever!" He reached for a can labeled "Persecution," but it turned out to be fuel. When he threw the fuel of persecution on the fire of Pentecost, there was a mighty explosion—an evangelism explosion! Soon there were even saints in Caesar's household. The Church spread everywhere. What was intended to stop the Church became the instrument of victory and progress. Persecution only gave the Christians new determination and impetus!

When it looked like the Church was ruined, the Holy Spirit took over. Like so many times through the centuries, what was intended for evil, God has a way of bringing out for good. He is never boxed in! In fact, God has a way of overruling: "Surely the wrath of man shall praise thee" (Ps. 76:10, KJV), exclaimed the Psalmist.

Everything which comes to His children has passed under God's stamp of censorship: "And God is faithful; he will not let you be tempted beyond what you can bear. But when you are tempted, he will also provide a way out so that you can stand up under it" (1 Cor. 10:13).

When Satan tries to stamp out the fire in our hearts, he only spreads the sparks! When all seems lost, God will make a way!

81

I. Out of the Ashes God
Resurrects New Life

The Church in Jerusalem had settled down into "business as usual." Its rapid growth following the weeks and months after Pentecost created a superchurch of thousands. However, after a couple of years, the intimacy of earlier days had faded and problems of assimilation set in. People started working on each other instead of on the devil, turning their attention to internal problems. They began to grumble and complain. Factions made an uneasy truce between Palestinian Jews and the Jews from Greek-speaking nations—both groups being Christians!

Under the leadership of the 11 apostles plus newly elected Matthias, organization had become necessary. The seven deacons selected and ordained as Church board members were all Hellenistic Christians—foreigners, if you please! Old-line Hebrew Christians couldn't handle the new, emerging leadership of the newcomer outsiders. It seems these Greek-speaking laymen were taking the initiative in the Church.

As Barker noted, "A few even began to grumble that the Greek-speaking Christians were starting to 'take over' the church."[3] Commenting further, he wrote: "Although no one realized it at the time, the leadership of the church shifted from the Apostles and 'Hebrews' to these energetic, imaginative young men. From this point on in Acts, the importance of Jerusalem dims. Stephen's martyrdom burst the church from its temple husk, exploding his associates into Samaria, Judea, the Philistine coast, Antioch, Cyprus, Asia Minor—even Europe."[4]

At a time when things might be getting a bit stale, along came the unexpected persecution intending to stamp out what fire was left. Surely the death of the Church was imminent! But looking back over the centuries, "every time the world has cleared its throat to pronounce the church dead, the Spirit has stirred the body to startling new life."[5]

Only when the church is patronized, made official, given popular approval and acceptance does it go dead and stale. But the Church of Jesus Christ springs up from persecution with new life and vigor and enthusiasm.

From what was assumed to be the ashes of tragedy, the Spirit's new life began surging through the sleeping giant. Ray Stedman makes a brilliant observation:

> Yet God used Saul's rage to accomplish two things: He forced the church out of Jerusalem and He made the early church depend on the gifts which the Spirit distributed to *everyone*, instead of simply on the apostles' gifts . . . ordinary, plain-vanilla Christians who nevertheless had gifts of the Spirit. But they would never have discovered their gifts if God had not used this pressure to place them in circumstances where they had to develop the gifts of evangelism, witnessing, helps, wisdom, knowledge, teaching and prophecy—all gifts which the Spirit had made available to them.[6]

Instead of stamping out the flame, Saul and his men just spread the sparks of new life everywhere—Judea, Samaria, all over the Mediterranean world! Jesus' promise at His ascension was being fulfilled: "But you will receive power when the Holy Spirit comes on you; and you will be my witnesses in Jerusalem, and in all Judea and Samaria, and to the ends of the earth" (Acts 1:8).

Out of the ashes sprang new life that couldn't be extinguished. Tertullian, one of the Early Church fathers, remarked: "The blood of the martyrs is the seed of the Church."

Within the present decade, the African nation of Uganda has seen the bloody persecution of Christians under the government of Idi Amin. One of the great Christian leaders, Bishop Festo Kivengere, reflected on those Christians who have been faithful unto death. He wrote:

A living church cannot be destroyed by fire or by guns. The church is like our African grasslands, where I herded cattle as a boy. Huge fires roar over it, and the land looks black and dead. But immediately after the first rain, the grass springs up more luxuriantly than ever. The plains turn green and the cows fatten. No fire passing over the church can destroy the seeds of victorious faith. And the church in Uganda today is springing up, rich, green, and growing![7]

The church is not only a mothering community; it is also a ministering community. It is not just a gathered people; it must also be a scattered people. Like a harbor, the church is a fellowship into which people may come, but it must also be a fellowship where people are equipped to go out.

When pressures, problems, and people have done their best to stamp out the fire of the Spirit in one's own heart, it is good to remember that God will raise up an ever-renewing life!

II. OUT OF THE ASHES GOD SPREADS HIS KINGDOM

Luke wrote: "All except the apostles were scattered throughout Judea and Samaria. . . . Those who had been scattered preached the word wherever they went" (Acts 8:1, 4).

What seemed tragic for the Church became the catalyst for the expansion of the Church. Perhaps the Christians were having such a jolly time together in Jerusalem that it took persecution to drive them out! Obviously Luke considered the persecution and scattering as a very essential epoch in the history of the Early Church.

In an age without communication systems like radio, television, and jet airliners, the gospel of Christ spread like an epidemic from village to village, from city to city, from country to country. The men and women couldn't keep it a secret; they instinctively shared the Good News with relatives, friends, and neighbors. Doors of opportunity opened here and there. Persecution ended in proclamation!

Since Luke had been an "outsider," he didn't want the Church to forget its mission to strangers. By his design the Book of Acts traces the scattering of the sparks. To illustrate, Luke focuses the spread of the Church on one man— Philip. Not Philip the apostle, but Philip the deacon, the layman, the evangelist! He, like the rest, was running for his life. Apparently headed for his hometown of Caesarea, Philip traveled through Samaria. He seemed not so much looking for a place to hide as he did for a place to tell about Jesus Christ! The Pharisee "heresy hunters" hated Samaritans so much they were not apt to come through such unholy territory as Samaria.

Philip, not being a hidebound, old-line Jew, was not timid in proclaiming Christ to the half-breed Samaritans: "Philip went down to a city in Samaria and proclaimed the Christ there. When the crowds heard Philip and saw the miraculous signs he did, they all paid close attention to what he said" (Acts 8:5-6). The Greek text suggests Philip "heralded" the Good News, like one boldly trumpeting to make way for the King.

The Samaritans had been looking and longing for the Messiah. Their segregated lives were empty and futile. Out of the deep needs of their hearts was a desperate reach for truth. Like most of the Roman world, they ached for some great deliverance. And, as Philip preached Christ, there was an astounding response. A poet said it well: "I have preached philosophy and men have faltered; I have preached Christ and men have repented!"[8]

Out of the ashes of despair, the kingdom of God was spread naturally and spontaneously. Perhaps the Church until that moment had no concept of a world mission, but God was at work behind the scenes pushing the Church toward its destiny. Philip was quick to discover that Jesus Christ is for the whole world!

A neighboring pastor of the author commented:

> This was not point one in a carefully outlined strategy of the early church for the expansion of the fellowship to the world. Persecution prompted it; scattering motivated it. The followers of the resurrected Lord were equally amazed that their zeal for Christ superseded ancient prejudices. Without thinking about it, they shared the good news wherever they went. They couldn't help it. Their joy spilled over on Jews, half-breeds and Gentiles alike. . . . [Philip] simply found himself in Samaria and did what was now more natural than breathing, sleeping, or eating: he preached the love and forgiveness of Jesus Christ.[9]

While persecution scattered the sparks of Spirit-filled lives, it must be noted that the scattering happens best as each believer tells those near him, and they tell their friends in ever-widening circles. One writer stated: " 'A missionary does not necessarily go outside of his country, his state, or even his own community. A true missionary needs only to go outside himself.' That's all any church member needs to do to be a missionary: escape the prison of his self-consciousness and fear and declare even to his nearest neighbor the life he has found in Christ."[10]

A recent study by the Institute for American Church Growth indicates that people brought into the church by a relative or friend constitutes 70 to 80 percent of church growth. Perry Tanksley penned these words:

> Desiring to witness
>   I volunteered to preach,
> But Jesus said to me,
>   "Go witness on your street."
> "I seek a larger place,"
>   I pled in bold self-pity.
> "Then go," He whispered low,

"Go witness in your city."
"I mean elsewhere," I begged,
"Like some far-distant place;
Lord, here in my hometown
They'd laugh right in my face."

He wept, "But Judea mocked;
Galilee turned me down;
Jerusalem spit on me;
They laughed in my hometown."
Deeply touched, I went forth
To witness to my neighbor
Who welcomed and made me glad;
I dared to go and labor.
And I, surprised, soon learned
There are no distant places
With needs more deeply etched
Than on familiar faces.

When Dr. Beecher was pastor of Park Street Church, Boston, he was asked about the secret of his success there. He replied, "I preach on Sunday, but I have 450 members who take my message on Monday and preach it wherever they go!"[11]

While Satan was stamping on the fire, out of the ashes God spread His kingdom—until it has included each and every believer today!

III. Out of the Ashes God Demonstrates His Power

Luke continued: "When the crowds heard Philip and saw the miraculous signs he did, they all paid close attention to what he said. With shrieks, evil spirits came out of many, and many paralytics and cripples were healed" (Acts 8:6-7).

Not all preaching and witnessing is good news. Some are dismal lectures of doom and despair. Various sermons

I've heard remind me of a cartoon in my files. A forlorn character is watching television from which a voice resounds: ". . . In summation, the economic picture is worsening by the hour, the threat of armed conflict increases, experts predict worldwide famine within this decade, and scientists today announced that the earth is on the threshold of another glacial age. That's the news for tonight. Have a pleasant good evening!"

But not Philip the "good-newser"! He preached Christ —and the power of God honored the message with converts, changed lives, and healing of hearts and bodies and emotions! God reinforced the Good News by "the power of God for the salvation of everyone who believes: first for the Jew, then for the Gentile" (Rom. 1:16).

Preaching Christ is the message urging men to trust Christ's good work on the Cross for salvation. It is not exhorting men to "try hard to be good." There's no saving gospel in that; there's no power in that advice.

Halford Luccock wrote:

> Many years ago, when Kipling's poem, "If," had such a great vogue, a minister was speaking to a company of human derelicts, gathered in a rescue mission on a "Skid Row." He was urging his dreary audience to lift themselves to better living, and recited, in an unctuous, rotund voice, the whole of Kipling's [poem] "If," ending sonorously with the lines, "If you can fill the unforgiving minute with sixty seconds' worth of distance run." In the pause which followed, a voice came from a back seat, asking, "What if you can't?"[12]

People have pulled on their own bootstraps long enough to know they can't change their lives by themselves. The gospel, in the words of A. W. Tozer, "has been watered down until the solution is so weak that if it were poison it would not hurt anyone, and if it were medicine it would not cure anyone."

When Christ is proclaimed by one's life and lips, there is power in his witness! God is not maimed when His Church is pressured and persecuted. Out of the ashes, God demonstrates even today that He still performs miracles of grace—forgiving, cleansing, filling, empowering, healing!

IV. OUT OF THE ASHES GOD BRINGS GREAT JOY

As a result of persecution, Philip was driven from Jerusalem, passed over the border into Samaria, and brought the message of Christ. Luke describes the outcome simply: "So there was great joy in that city" (Acts 8:8).

It's always joyful when men turn to the living Lord, Jesus Christ. A natural consequence of God's power at work was a joy those Samaritans had never known before. Only counterfeit Christianity brings an atmosphere of gloom. Christ brings a radiant joy into people's lives!

Outward circumstances are not always changed, the pressures and problems and persecutions do not always dissolve, but people are filled with liberty and joy. The good news of Jesus does not make men melancholy but fills them with gladness. As Luke noted at the beginning of his first book, it is "good news of great joy that will be for all the people" (Luke 2:10).

What a powerful message the gospel must be! It brought hope and joy to even the despised people of Samaria. That's a dramatic change! God's heart revealed in Christ still offers hope, still reaches for the brokenhearted, the downcast, the lonely, the empty soul. If one's quest for happiness is threadbare, if one is at the end of his rope, here's Jesus! He gives great joy as He comes to reside within—at our invitation. Joy is the flag which flies above the castle of our heart when the King of Kings is in residence.

When Columbus returned to Europe from his amazing

discovery of the Americas, he had to prove he found another world. His most convincing evidence was a new kind of people—the American Indians whom he brought back with him. And Halford Luccock added, "The crowning evidence of Christianity is a new kind of people!"

When Satan tried to stamp out the fire of the Spirit, he just scattered the sparks of holy love and great joy all over God's beautiful world. And a new kind of people spring up wherever the sparks have flown.

7

Not for Sale—
At Any Price!

Acts 8:9-25

One man's evaluation of the church today is thought-provoking: "If God called His Holy Spirit out of the world, about 95 percent of what we are doing would go right on—and we would brag about it."

A. C. Dixon reminds us: "When we rely on organization, we get what organization can do. When we rely upon education, we get what education can do. When we rely upon eloquence, we get what eloquence can do. When we rely on the Holy Spirit, we get what God can do!"

This is in similar vein to the words of E. M. Bounds: "What the Church needs today is not more machinery or better, not new organizations or more and novel methods, but men whom the Holy Ghost can use—men of prayer, men mighty in prayer."[1]

What the church needs most—and must have—is the Holy Spirit. We cannot buy Him. He is not for sale. We cannot earn Him. He is the free gift of grace. We cannot coerce Him. He is God's response to our surrender.

In the midst of the Samaritan revival, the power of the Holy Spirit was made evident by great joy. Simon the magician, known as the Great Power, lost his following as people responded to the good news about Jesus Christ. Luke pens the strange story of Simon who decided, "If you can't lick 'em, join 'em!" Simon moved into Christian circles and yearned for the mysterious but effective power of the Holy Spirit.

His quest for the power of the Spirit teaches important lessons about the Holy Spirit. Simon's futile efforts to gain God's Spirit has a familiar ring. But the Holy Spirit is not for sale—at any price!

I. Simon Experienced Conformity

Outward conformity is the wrong approach to the Spirit. When Simon saw his Samaritan followers believing Philip's message of the kingdom of God and being baptized, he went with them and tried to conform to their new ways.

Simon gave outward conformity by believing in the power of Jesus. Luke simply wrote: "Simon himself believed" (Acts 8:13). There's no evidence that Simon's faith was a saving faith. Having seen "the great signs and miracles" (ibid.), Simon was convinced that the name of Jesus was a powerful charm. His "belief" was mental assent, not moral consent, not heart commitment. James wrote: "You believe that there is one God. Good! Even the demons believe that—and shudder" (Jas. 2:19). There is a belief without submission of the will!

An inadequate faith merely rejoices in signs and wonders. It is a "shallow, emotional response, without the deep moral surrender of self which is the essence of saving faith."[2] If a man is told there are 300 billion stars in the universe, he will believe it. However, if he is told a bench has just been painted, he has to touch it to be sure. The Bible teaches a belief which learns to trust without touching! A lot of religious "believism" has no deep, abiding trust in God's integrity.

What a blow to the Christian worker when he discovers his converts have not really had a change of mind and conduct—only a change of creed! One writer described the multitude of Simons today:

> Our churches are overloaded with claiming "Christians" who do not live the evidence of their profession. These so-called converts of "believe-only" evangelism have become the biggest heartache of the church. They must constantly be prodded to live the kind of life that they are totally incapable of producing. Christian life conferences do not cause them to live a genuine Christian life; soul winning seminars do not make soul winners of them. They are the "dead wood" of the church. Religiously, they merely exist without the reality of regeneration.[3]

Simon gave outward conformity by being baptized. Just because Simon was baptized, one must not conclude Simon was actually born again. One can go down into the water a dry sinner and merely come up a wet sinner! Baptism is the sacramental requirement of all new Christians, but there is no inherent moral boost except in obedient response to God's Word.

Philip had no way to see into Simon's heart. Only God knows the heart. The genuinely repentant sinner looks just like the one who takes it lightly—at first. One must simply hope for the best. The church has always had good and bad members. Jesus said the church is like a net catching good and bad fish. In God's great day of judgment, He alone will sort out the good from the bad (Matt. 13:47-50).

Simon gave outward conformity by becoming a backer of Philip. "And he followed Philip everywhere, astonished by the great signs and miracles he saw" (Acts 8:13). Surely, Simon thought, this man Philip must have something going for him. He must be the answer to building a great congregation in Samaria! So Simon became one of his adherents. He went to all the meetings wherever Philip went. And, even today, "men get into a church without being reborn, but they don't get into *the* Church. They don't get into the body of Christ."[4] Simon said the right words. He conformed to all the outward sacraments and ceremonies. He learned to say the right things—but he was unchanged!

Dr. Lloyd Ogilvie wrote:

> It's possible to hear the gospel, take part in church activities, and be a faithful contributor without the experience of a vital living relationship with the Spirit of God. We can pray prayers without talking to God; we can teach and learn truth without being transformed by the truth; we can work for Christian causes without being healed ourselves; we can read the Bible and live with messed-up relationships; we can hear about the power of the Spirit and live inhibited, intransient lives.[5]

No, outward conformity is never an avenue to the Spirit of God.

II. Simon Experienced Confusion

Simon had wrong ideas about the Spirit. He seemed to view the Holy Spirit as a force, an impersonal power, a dramatic effect, a supernatural energy—something one might bargain for.

Today there is an abundance of cheap ideas and twisted concepts of who the Holy Spirit is and what His filling accomplishes. In describing the filling of the Holy Spirit, one writer tried to clarify it: "Not to make me bubbly and exuberant. Not to set an example of my good behavior. Not to prove that Christians are happier than anybody else. Not to bring about world peace. But to make me a loving person whose love would glorify the God of love."

Simon thought the Spirit was power apart from purity. John T. Seamands wrote with discernment:

> Simon Magus thought of the baptism of the Holy Spirit as an end in itself. He thought of Pentecost in terms of power to do the showy, the spectacular thing.

. . . He wanted to make an impression on the people. He was more concerned about his *conquests* than his *character;* more concerned about what he was going to *do* than what he was going to *be.* He wanted the Holy Spirit so that he could use the Spirit, not so that the Spirit could use him. He wanted to glorify *self,* not the *Saviour.*[6]

As I prepared for this unique study, the Holy Spirit shined His searchlight through my heart. It was not a quick flash, but the slow, all-seeing scan of God through my soul: "Why do I want the power of the Holy Spirit in my life? That I may be Christlike? Or that I might be effective and capable of influencing people? Why do I want to influence people for the Kingdom? For their good—or mine?" Let's never forget: The Holy Spirit is not given to make us great or wise, but to make us good and pure! When we're honest before God, we begin to see there's always the danger of playing with Christian truth rather than practicing it!

We are not to seek power—but God's purity. Power is only the by-product of obedience to God's delicate voice. Instead of praying for power, we ought to pray for the Holy Spirit's cleansing and control! We are just like Simon if we simply want the Holy Spirit so we can do something wonderful and great.

Simon thought the Spirit was given by the methods of men. Peter and John were sent up to the Samaritan revival to check things out. Luke notes: "When they arrived, they prayed for them that they might receive the Holy Spirit, because the Holy Spirit had not yet come upon any of them; they had simply been baptized into the name of the Lord Jesus. Then Peter and John placed their hands on them, and they received the Holy Spirit.

"When Simon saw that the Spirit was given at the laying on of the apostles' hands, he offered them money . . ." (Acts 8:15-18).

At first Simon thought water baptism was the answer. But now he watched the apostles laying on their hands. And he wanted that powerful touch! Simon thought he would try to use their methods. The laying on of hands was an ancient custom of blessing. It would seem appropriate to reduplicate that method—so Simon thought.

And the church of our day has its methods. Within the custom of the Church of the Nazarene, people seeking the Holy Spirit are urged to come forward and kneel at the "mourner's bench," known in recent years as "the altar." What a wonderful time and place to receive God's greatest gift—the gift of the Spirit! However, some have watched and then made that second trip to the altar as though the coming is the receiving. There is no magic in coming to the altar. It is only a convenient place to pray, to receive the counsel of pastors and concerned laymen, to allow brothers in Christ to pray for the seeker and with the seeker. God's power is not in the method—but in the reality of the Holy Spirit's cleansing and filling of the open and receptive heart and life!

Simon thought the Spirit could be earned by doing something. Luke adds, "When Simon saw that the Spirit was given at the laying on of the apostles' hands, he offered them money and said, 'Give me also this ability so that everyone on whom I lay my hands may receive the Holy Spirit'" (Acts 8:18-19). Being a magician by vocation, Simon, no doubt, had paid dearly to other magicians for the ability to perform various tricks and magical stunts. That's why magicians don't tell their tricks—they sell them. It is part of their business and stock-in-trade. Simon thought surely there must be a price for that amazing ability to bestow the Holy Spirit by laying on of hands.

Incidentally, this man gave the term *simony* to religious vocabularies. The dictionary defines *simony:* "(1) the making of money out of sacred things. (2) sin of buying or selling positions, promotions, etc., in the church."

The Holy Spirit cannot be purchased with money. He cannot be purchased by self-effort or good works. He cannot be purchased with tears or lengthy prayers. He cannot be purchased with anything. The Holy Spirit is the gift of God to all His children who will accept Him.

Simon thought the Spirit could be obtained by offering less than full surrender. To be filled with the Holy Spirit, one must make a total and complete surrender of himself to God. The giving of the Spirit is God's response to one's self-surrender to the Lordship of Jesus Christ!

Some people have been trying for years to find the reality of the Spirit-filled life. Many have been nibbling around the edges of the really sanctified life, trying in one form or another to get by God without 100 percent total surrender to the Master. And they'll never know the joy of the Lord until they give Him the whole works—family, possessions, position, and inner self. It's all—or nothing! They will never have the blessing of God until they really mean, "I surrender all! I surrender all!"

One of my parishioners, Ed Treece, loaned me a tape from his Amway business which reminded me so much of the way many, many sad Christians dabble with God's Holy Spirit. The speech was by Rich De Vos, president of Amway, entitled "Try or Cry":

> Some of you remind me of a fellow I used to sponsor. He lived out in the great state of Montana. He was a wonderful fellow—tall, good-looking guy, had a family. He used to sign all his letters: "Your western horizon"! That was before we had a distributor west of Grand Rapids anywhere. Always he would write these beautiful letters every week and say: "Dear Rich: This week we are going to get back on the road to success. But the only problem is—my mother-in-law came to visit. I've got to show her around the mountains. But as soon as she leaves, we will be back on the main high-

way to success." He would always sign his letters: "Your western horizon."

And it always was followed by a "P.S. Please hold the check one week."

The following week this guy writes: "Dear Rich: This is the week we were going to go. We just discovered, however, that my wife is pregnant. Now I've got to get the room done upstairs. But as soon as I get that finished, I'm going to get out and make those calls, get me some customers, start holding some meetings, and we'll be back on the main road to success! Sincerely, Your western horizon. P.S. Please hold the check for two weeks."

Well, the following week, the letter would come. "Dear Rich: I'm sorry, but this week I'm off on the shoulder of the road again. But as soon as we get the house painted, and get that thing done, I'll be back on the main road to success. P.S. Please hold your check. Your western horizon."

His series of letters ran for two solid years. Always, "Your western horizon." Always some problem got in his way. It was either his car was broken down and he had to fix it. Or something was wrong with the house. Or something was wrong with the weather—a snowstorm came, or it was too hot! He had to take the family on a vacation. He was always saying, "Now I am on the detour, but when I get off this detour, I'll be on the main road."

Sometimes he was on the side road. Sometimes he was on the shoulder. He never got on the road to success. His last letter said: "P.S. Please hold the check for two weeks after you ship me the soap."

Wonderful guy—but no commitment.

Is one tired of spiritual detours? He needs God's wonderful Holy Spirit—and he knows that! He must quit fooling around, attempting to offer God less than total surrender!

III. SIMON EXPERIENCED CONFRONTATION

As evidenced by what he said and did, Simon had a wrong relationship with God.

Simon's heart was not right with God: "Peter answered: 'May your money perish with you, because you thought you could buy the gift of God with money! You have no part or share in this ministry, because your heart is not right before God. Repent of this wickedness and pray to the Lord. Perhaps he will forgive you for having such a thought in your heart. For I see that you are full of bitterness and captive to sin" (Acts 8:20-23).

Peter confronted Simon and exposed him to himself. Peter stabbed right at the heart of the problem: "Your heart is not right before God." He saw Simon's motives. He saw the heart full of self and sin. Simon never had been set free! No wonder many have never received the Holy Spirit —they have never been converted. Jesus warned: "The world cannot accept [this Counselor], because it neither sees him nor knows him. But you know him, for he lives with you and will be in you" (John 14:17).

The test of genuine conversion is: "Did something happen in my life, a real change in my life?"

Simon's heart was still self-centered. He wanted divine power and privilege. Simon had not died to Simon. Simon ruled the throne of Simon's heart. He was not yearning for the presence of the Spirit, but for power to affect other people's lives. Some folk are only happy when they direct the orchestra from the podium. They're never content to play the oboe or second violin! Myron Augsburger noted: "They sin against the Spirit in seeking to get His comfort without yielding to His control!"[7]

God will reveal to one his own heart enthroned by self. Nothing ought to bring him quicker to the feet of Jesus.

Former Congressman Brooks Hays told of a bishop who advised a politician to go out into the rain and lift his head heavenward. "It will bring a revelation to you."

The next day the politician reported, "I followed your

advice and no revelation came. The water poured down my neck, and I felt like a fool."

"Well," said the bishop, "isn't that quite a revelation for the first try?"

Simon's heart was not yielded to God. When Peter confronted him with God's judgments on insincerity, "Then Simon answered, 'Pray to the Lord for me so that nothing you have said may happen to me' " (Acts 8:24).

Interestingly, Simon didn't repent. He only wanted to escape the penalty for his neglect and insincerity. Simon was saying, according to Ogilvie: "Friend,—I can't—I won't—change, but pray that the Lord won't judge me and will bless me anyhow!"[8] There's no hint of repentance—only regret! There's no thirsting after righteousness or longing for fellowship with God's Spirit.

Refusing to make such a beautiful, full surrender to God, Simon's life became a tragedy. Here was his opportunity for abundant life—but he didn't take that important step of faith! According to the apocryphal books, Simon Magus hindered the gospel everywhere he went. In Rome he gathered a large following of people known even into the third century A.D. as the "Simonians."

In fact, strong church tradition claims Simon was worshipped in Rome, and in an effort to perform one last great miracle, he had his disciples bury him alive for three days. When they opened his grave, he was dead. What a pitiful ending for a man who came so close to God's truth, so close to the great movings of the Holy Spirit, and refused to give total surrender to the Lordship of Jesus.

The sailors with Christopher Columbus watched native American Indians bouncing a crude ball made out of a strange substance from trees. They had great fun watching the toy. They just didn't know what they were looking at —it was rubber.

Samuel Colt, inventor of the Colt .45 revolver, used to

play with a little machine which gave electric shocks to adventurous customers for 10c a jolt. He didn't know what he was playing with.

Dr. Long in Athens, Ga., conducted "laughing gas" parties with people inhaling and experiencing an exhilaration. Today people face surgery every day upheld by anesthesia.

After the first three centuries of the Church, religion was treated like a toy. They just didn't know what they had in the potential of the Holy Spirit. Halford Luccock wrote: "Here is Gibbon's tremendous indictment of the monks of Constantinople, the sterile pedants of the tenth century: 'They held in their lifeless hands the riches of their fathers, without inheriting the spirit which had created that sacred patrimony. They read; they praised; they compiled; but their languid souls seemed alike incapable of action and thought.' Their faith was an antique—not a power!"[9]

What is the Holy Spirit to us? An antique or a power? If somehow we could only grasp that He is available to us today, what a fantastic discovery would take place in our souls, in the heart of the church!

Charles Allen told of

an old Chinese tale about a little fish who once overheard one fisherman say to another, "Have you ever stopped to think how essential water is to life? Without water our earth would dry up. Everything would die."

The fish became panic-stricken. "I must find some water at once! If not, in a few days I will be dead." And the fish went swimming away as fast as he could. But where could he find water? He had never heard of it before.

He asked other fish in the lake, but they didn't know. He swam out into a large river, but no fish there could tell him where to find water. He kept swimming until he reached the deepest place in the ocean. There he found an old and wise fish. He gasped, "Where can I find water?"

The old fish chuckled. "Water? Why you are in it right now. You were in it back home in your own lake. You have never been out of it since the day you were born."

The little fish began the long swim back home saying, "I had water all the time, and I didn't know it."[10]

When one is converted, born again, forgiven of his sins, the Holy Spirit has been in him and with him. But God desires to fill him with himself. Man's response is surrender. The Holy Spirit doesn't have to come from anywhere. He is right there today and is being offered to the surrendered child of God as God's greatest Gift.

A young pastor spoke with Dr. Charles Strickland one night. He testified, "Dr. Strickland, I came through the church and through all of its processes of education. I have heard holiness preached; I have listened to it. I have heard people testify. I have never been able to feel that I really had the Holy Spirit. I know the theology of the church. I have studied it."

Then he paused, and with tears filling his eyes, he went on: "It came to me so beautifully and so simply just the other day—what the Lord was really trying to do in filling me with His Spirit. I must simply open my heart and mind to Him. I went out in the woods the other day and said, 'God, I will be Your man and You furnish the grace.' And He filled me.

"I have sought it. I have studied it. I have wanted it. I have asked for it. Sir, I finally found it when I just turned loose and let God have me. I had some ambitions. I had some plans. I had some things which I thought were important to me, some sacred things—and I had to turn them loose. When I did, He came!"

We can't buy the Holy Spirit with the whole world, but He will be given to us as we give God our whole self!

102

8

A Man
Under Orders

Acts 8:26-40

A few years ago, an evangelist named George Watmough told this story:

> I was waiting for a ride in San Jose, California. All of a sudden a car stopped in front of me. A lady was sitting there, and she asked, "Would you like a ride?" To put us both at ease, I told her that I was a Christian and that I loved the Lord. I began to talk to her about spiritual matters.
>
> Finally, after about fifteen minutes, she turned to me and said, "Isn't it strange that I should have picked you up? I don't know how many people I've passed, but something seemed to say, 'Pick that man up.' Just this morning I was listening to a preacher on the radio. He was talking just the way you are. When he finished, I wrote something in this book."
>
> She reached over and took a little red book out of her bag. This is what it said: "What I need is God. How can I find Him?" I knew then that God had placed me there to bring her the good news of salvation.[1]

How like the experience of Philip the deacon in Acts 8! Without a doubt Philip was "a man under orders." Hitchhiking on the desert Gaza road, Philip had one of those beautiful "divine appointments" which comes so often—and is recognized so seldom! Being under God's orders, Philip was easy to get moving and was sensitive to God's stopping places. A man of influence and power in Ethiopia was hungry for God, and Philip was the right man at the right place at the right time—a man under orders!

The church, since the dawn of Christianity, has always been at its best when it has been the most militantly evangelistic. That's when it has made the greatest efforts to expand, but that's when it has been most refined by opposition and persecution. However, in such times has come a fierce dedication to take the Good News to every man at any cost!

Persecution had sent the Christians scattering throughout the Mediterranean world. Headed for home, Philip told of Jesus everywhere; as a result a great Samaritan revival took place. Right in the middle of overwhelming success, the Lord changed Philip's orders. He sent him from the masses to a divine appointment in the desert Gaza road to meet one man.

As Helen Temple editorialized: "If you're looking for adventure, try the will of God. Total commitment is an open door to the impossible, the unbelievable, and the unexpected. . . . The mark of God is that He leads you where you didn't plan to go."[2]

Philip is described by Bonhoeffer's statement: "Only he who believes obeys, and only he who obeys believes!" What is seen in this obedient layman's life is desperately needed today: "The same vision: the mobilizing and equipping of the vast lay army of the church to do the work of ministry. It seems that after centuries of a clergy-oriented ministry the Holy Spirit is finally breaking through our man-made molds to create the type of church that He meant should exist from the beginning, and which did exist for the first three centuries of this era of our Lord."[3]

It is my deepest prayer that each of us will also be "men under orders," on call for divine service.

I. Philip Had a Fascination for God's Guidance

Philip was on call and sensitive to the Spirit's voice: "Now an angel of the Lord said to Philip, 'Go south to the road—the desert road—that goes down from Jerusalem to Gaza'" (Acts 8:26).

In the first introduction of Philip, he was numbered with those candidates for lay leadership as one "full of the Spirit" (6:3). Since God's Spirit controlled him, Philip was eager and sensitive to His guidance.

For one thing, Philip listened *for* the Spirit's orders. He had put himself under divine direction. He was tuned in to the Spirit's voice in his life. Philip had an ear for the promptings of God. When one door closes, God opens another door —but we often look so longingly and regretfully at the closed door, we do not see the door God has opened for us now. H. Cunliffe Jones said, "The guidance of the Holy Spirit does not come to a passive mind, but is a supernatural enrichment of an active one."

Dr. E. Stanley Jones wrote:

> As a friend put it: "I cannot always trust my guidance, but I can always trust my Guide." Don't lose faith in [God] if guidance goes wrong; lose faith in your method of guidance and reexamine it.
>
> But if we are honest, basically honest, the guidance will seldom go wrong. Then tune yourself to hear His voice. He is the God who speaks.
>
> A Quaker woman inquired of a young man she knew: "Hast thou heard God speak lately?" And when he answered, "No," she commented: "Thee must have forgotten to be still." "Be still and know;" be unstill and you will not know. God guides everyone who really wants to be guided.[4]

Mrs. Gordon T. Olsen reminisced:

> We walked through the beautiful field of grain on my sister and brother-in-law's farm in Idaho. Spot, the pointer dog, followed close by, running zigzag, sniffing, searching. Suddenly the dog froze in a rigid position—tail straight, nose pointing—there it was! His prey—a pheasant. We walked on. The dog ran far ahead, jumped a creek, and hunted through the tules quite a distance away. My brother-in-law whistled for the dog to come back—"He must not run too far ahead of me, but must learn to stay by my side, to hear my command."[5]

One needs to ask himself, "Am I staying close enough to God to hear His commands and to sense His guidance?"

For another thing, Philip listened *to* the Spirit's voice: "Go south to the road—the desert road—that goes down from Jerusalem to Gaza" (Acts 8:26). It was 35 miles from Samaria to Jerusalem; another 60 miles farther on down to Gaza—probably on foot! William Barclay explains: "There were two Gazas. Gaza had been destroyed in war in 93 B.C. and a new Gaza had been built to the south in 57 B.C. The first Gaza was called Old or Desert Gaza to distinguish it from the other. This road which led by Gaza would be a road where the traffic of half the world went by."[6]

Philip was enjoying the great revival in Samaria, but there came a sudden turn of direction. Since Philip always kept a listening ear to the Spirit, he heard exactly what the Spirit said to him. Other friends probably questioned such a strange move, "Are you sure God wants you to go to the desert?" As one put it: "Does the sudden shift in His orders seem so abrupt that you hesitate and argue that it doesn't make sense? Ah, but His ways are not ours. If He sends you to the desert He can furnish streams of water there."[7]

Since Philip had a fascination for God's guidance, he was obedient to the Spirit's voice. Philip moved under the inspiration and motivation of the Holy Spirit. One writer said: "I want to share with you what I believe is the secret of an exciting life. People who have discovered it are some of the most attractive, winsome people I know. They sparkle and shine with an identifiable radiance. Their lives are distinguished by an eagerness and earnestness. They have zeal and zest. . . . The mysterious origin of this vitality is traceable to two words: *guidance* and *obedience*."[8]

The Bible says of Philip, "So he started out" (Acts 8:27).

He accepted orders immediately; it was instant obedience. That's the dynamic of Christian living—immediate response: "Yes, Lord! Yes, Lord!" Had Philip delayed, he would have missed his divine appointment—the right man at the right place at the wrong time! In retrospect, one needs to ask himself: "Have I ever been there—at the wrong time—because I procrastinated? Have I missed God's timing because I waited for the 'big opportunity'?"

God didn't have to explain "why" to Philip; he accepted orders unconditionally! He gave unquestioned obedience. Philip didn't need to know why he was going. Trusting God completely, he knew God must have a good reason.

Spiritual success requires consecration without reservation! It is well to remember: "Philip had a date with the eunuch and didn't know it. If God orders you out on the lone road, He has a date for you to keep with someone, maybe with some bewildered soul, maybe with Himself. . . . As you obey, you may not see the *why* of it, but you shall see the *Who*. He who says 'Go' goes along."[9]

Such unquestioned, instant obedience to God is also for one's own good. Donald J. Barnhouse told this story:

In the Belgian Congo, the weather was hot and dank. No breath of air stirred; leaves hung from the trees as though they were weighted. In the garden not far from the missionary home a small boy played under a tree. Suddenly, the father called to him: "Philip, obey me instantly—get down on your stomach." The boy reacted at once, and his father continued, "Now crawl toward me fast." The boy again obeyed. After he had come about halfway, the father said, "Now stand up and run to me." The boy reached his father and turned to look back. Hanging from the branch under which he had been playing was a 15-foot serpent.

Are we always as ready to obey? Or do we say: "Tell me why? Explain to me? I will after a while." Let it be, "Speak, Lord, thy servant hears."[10]

God didn't outline the whole program for Philip—just the first step. That's often how God leads—one step at a time.

> . . . *Lead Thou me on!*
> *Keep Thou my feet; I do not ask to see*
> *The distant scene; one step enough for me.*
>
> —JOHN H. NEWMAN, 1801-90

A pastor was driving home when suddenly he had an urge to stop at a big house on the corner. He knew nothing about the people in that house, so he didn't want to do anything foolish—and he drove on. However, the Spirit's voice seemed to prompt him with urgency, so he turned around and went back.

When the old man met him at the door and learned he was the local pastor, he burst into tears. That unknown old man was a backslidden preacher. He had been away from God for many years. Desperately he and his wife had been trying to get back to God. In fact, that very morning they had prayed that if there was any hope for them, a preacher would be sent to them that day. The old man admitted finally he had planned to commit suicide if no one came.

What if no one had been living close enough to God to hear the Spirit's voice and to obey immediately without question? Are we, too, under orders?

Since Philip was fascinated with God's guidance, he was responsive to the Spirit's voice: "So he started out, and on his way he met an Ethiopian eunuch, an important official in charge of all the treasury of Candace, queen of the Ethiopians. This man had gone to Jerusalem to worship, and on his way home was sitting in his chariot reading the book of Isaiah the prophet. The Spirit told Philip, 'Go to that chariot and stay near it.' Then Philip ran up to the chariot" (Acts 8:27-30). Dr. Lloyd Ogilvie quoted R. H. L. Sheppard: "Christianity does not consist in abstaining from doing things no gentleman would think of doing, but in doing things that are unlikely to occur to anyone who is not in touch with the Spirit of Christ."[11]

Philip recognized God's appointment. Since the Holy Spirit directed this drama, He got Philip to the right place at the right time to meet the right man! And the same Spirit who got Philip there guided him in the encounter: "Go to that chariot and stay near it" (v. 29). Evangelism at its best is not hit-and-miss, but going under God's direction, having a divine appointment, and sticking with that person with love. God wants our availability more than our ability.

Philip not only recognized God's appointment, he also responded to God's assignment: "Then Philip ran up to the chariot" (v. 30). There's just no time lag between God's command and Philip's response of obedience. And where God guides, God provides! One must learn to be responsive to the promptings of the Spirit so often given in practical ways: "Say this; write that letter; make that phone call; send that gift; make that visit; do that act out of love with no thought of reward."[12]

A young single adult woman told her pastor: "Now that I believe God can plant thoughts in my mind, I have begun to follow orders. I can hardly believe the results. When I am guided to speak to people and say what I am led to say, they keep responding, 'That's just what I need to hear today!' The other day I called a friend who was on my mind. He was in deep trouble. 'How did you know I was having problems?' he asked. I didn't know, but I felt I had to call.'' [13]

We have a tendency to discount what God asks us to do for just one person. We seem to think it must be for a group or it isn't spiritual enough. But God sent Philip 95 miles one way to meet just one man.

Back during the Civil War, Southern Baptist Theological Seminary had to close its doors until the fighting was over. In November of 1865, it was reopened—but with only seven students and four professors. In the face of overwhelming odds, those four professors covenanted with God to give that school their life if need be.

Dr. John A. Broadus had only one student in his class on preaching—one blind boy. Most people would have closed the class or been tempted to give it less than their best. But not Dr. Broadus. He did such a thorough job of preparing the class for that one student that his written notes became known among preachers for more than 100 years as the famous textbook, *The Preparation and Delivery of Sermons.*

Philip was sensitive, obedient, and responsive to the Spirit's voice.

II. PHILIP HAD A FAMILIARITY WITH GOD'S MESSAGE

Luke related it vividly:

Then Philip ran up to the chariot and heard the man reading Isaiah the prophet. "Do you understand what you are reading?" Philip asked.

"How can I," he said, "unless someone explains it to me?" So he invited Philip to come up and sit with him.

The eunuch was reading this passage of Scripture:

"He was led like a sheep to the
    slaughter,

> *and as a lamb before the shearer is*
> *silent,*
> *so he did not open his mouth.*
> *In his humiliation he was deprived*
> *of justice.*
> *Who can speak of his descendants?*
> *For his life was taken from the*
> *earth."*

The eunuch asked Philip, "Tell me, please, who is the prophet talking about, himself or someone else?" Then Philip began with that very passage of Scripture and told him the good news about Jesus *(Acts 8:30-35).*

Philip recognized the man's need. The man in the chariot was the secretary of the treasury under the Candace or queen of Ethiopia. Probably he had become a proselyte into the Jewish faith and had made his pilgrimage to Jerusalem for one of the great festivals. He had gone there to worship, but the empty rituals and sacrifices left him spiritually bankrupt. Surrounded by the wealth of a kingdom, he was still a pauper in his soul. Philip found him reading the expensive handwritten scrolls. As was the custom of that area, he read the Scriptures aloud—but Philip could detect an uncertain sound in his voice. Even the searching of the Scriptures had not yet brought him to any deep fulfillment. Everything about him had the echo of discontent.

Philip sensed the hunger of his heart and asked, "Do you understand what you are reading?" (v. 30).

Finding him reading Isaiah 53—of all chapters—Philip reviewed God's Word. What a beautiful thing when we can begin to apply the healing of God's Word to the hurting of man's need! God speaks through the Bible to men's hearts. It is up-to-date.

A certain librarian asked the head of the college science department to go through the science textbooks in the library to see which ones should be discarded. The science professor replied, "Any science textbook over 10 years old should be thrown out!"

But, by contrast, the Bible has lasted through the centuries and speaks yet in our day to human need. We must be Bible-centered in our study, in our teaching, and in our living demonstrations. Bible preaching and Bible reading are some of the catalysts for a great spiritual awakening! Without the Bible, religion is a grave.

In her style of simplicity, Helen Temple writes:

"Do you understand what that book is about?"

"How can I, unless someone explains it to me?" the man answered. "Get in, won't you, and tell me about it. Is this man talking about himself or someone else?"

How's that for a wide-open door?

I suppose Philip could have said, "Well, no, the prophet is not talking about himself, but it's a little hard to explain it to you."

But this was the desert. The man was headed south. He might never be in touch with the gospel again. Besides, God had sent him to meet this man. He couldn't sidestep his responsibility. He didn't want to. He jumped into the conversation like a hungry fish after bait. Taking the portion of Isaiah the Ethiopian was reading, Philip preached Jesus to him.[14]

When the learned clergymen of London quizzed Dwight L. Moody, an American lay evangelist, someone asked the inevitable: "Mr. Moody, what is your creed?" That question was always designed to provoke debates and confrontations.

Quietly, Moody answered: "My creed is in print."

The barking voices clamored: "Where? What's the name of the book?" People reached for pencils and pads to write down the unknown title.

Moody replied: "Isaiah 53:5—'But he was wounded for our transgressions, he was bruised for our iniquities: the chastisement of our peace was upon him; and with his stripes we are healed'" (KJV).

And Philip spelled out that same creed; he revealed Jesus' atonement. For the very first time the great Suffering Servant passage of Isaiah 53 is used as a text for Jesus' life, death, and resurrection. Jesus is our Suffering Servant whose death on the Cross mysteriously brings us life everlasting. Philip had a clear concept of Jesus as our Atonement for sin.

A man asked Dr. R. T. Williams, "Why did Jesus Christ die on the Cross? What was the object of His death? I don't have time for a sermon, so just in one simple statement give me a reason for Jesus' death."

Many things flashed across Dr. Williams' mind as he began the process of mental elimination, grasping for a central truth, a final word. He replied: "The object of the Atonement is to bring man into fellowship with God!"

Philip, using the Scriptures, not only told *about* Jesus, but gave a personal introduction *to* Jesus. That's the power of a personal witness!

W. E. Sangster wrote:

> A friend of mine had a comrade in the war who went into the shell-torn battlefield and brought back a wounded man. As he drew the groaning man to safety, he was fatally wounded himself. He knew before he died that the man he had rescued would live, and it was a great comfort to him as his own life ebbed away. At the last, half in delirium, he kept murmuring: "I brought him through. . . . I brought him through. . . ."
>
> Look at the Cross. Look at the flowing wounds. [Jesus] brought us through![15]

Philip, a man under orders, had a fascination for God's guidance and a familiarity with God's message.

III. PHILIP HAD A FELLOWSHIP IN GOD'S FAMILY

Luke continued: "As they traveled along the road, they came to some water and the eunuch said, 'Look, here is water. Why shouldn't I be baptized?' And he ordered the chariot to stop. Then both Philip and the eunuch went down into the water and Philip baptized him. When they came up out of the water, the Spirit of the Lord suddenly took Philip away, and the eunuch did not see him again, but went on his way rejoicing" (Acts 8:36-39).

Philip knew the scope of fellowship with God's family. All those born of the Spirit were God's family. Philip seems to have viewed the universality of the gospel before any of the other Christians. He had been the first to preach to the half-breed Samaritans, and now he makes the first introduction of Jesus to a man outside the Semitic race. He saw that all men, whosoever will, may come into the family of God. There are no barriers of race, rank, region, or religious background. God's family includes all of God's children: "Red and yellow, black and white; / They are precious in His sight!" The Spirit may have picked Philip for this important assignment because Philip was a Greek-cultured Jew and had not grown up with the narrow sectarian view of the Palestinian Jews.

Philip knew the source of fellowship for God's family. Fellowship was built on belief in Jesus. "Philip said, If thou believest with all thine heart, thou mayest. And he answered and said, I believe that Jesus Christ is the Son of God" (Acts 8:37, KJV). And our unity as companions is built on that belief. It is our foundation for building the Church of Jesus Christ!

Josef Meier of the Passion Play testified:

> One evening when I was playing the part of the Christus, as I had done many times before, and on a night when there were very few people in the audience and hope was running low, I came to the lines in the play where Jesus says, "Why take ye thought for the morrow, O ye of little faith!" I had said these words many, many times. They were part of my performance, a portion of the Master's words to His disciples. On this

particular night I heard myself say this line as I had often done, but something happened. For the first time, I asked myself, "Josef Meier, why don't you have the will to believe these words with all your heart? Don't just say them. Believe them!"

Like a flash it dawned upon me that I had been playing the part of Christ without actually believing as He believed or living the faith as He lived it. I don't know whether the spectators that night noticed anything new in my interpretation. I don't know whether they sensed that I paused momentarily at this point, but something was happening to me. Belief, trust, conviction came to me and from that moment on a change took place in everything.

Marcus Bach commented:

I could not help but wonder how often we "play the role of the Christus," speak His words, hear His words, and even imagine ourselves suffering as He suffered, and never have the will to believe that His words are words of life. Josef Meier in his superb enactment of this delicate and important characterization even hangs upon a literal cross as the Christus did, but the "miracle" came only when he suddenly not merely played the part, but believed it![16]

The eunuch's belief in Jesus cemented him and Philip in bonds of love within God's family—which includes us today!

Philip knew the symbol of fellowship into God's family. That symbol is baptism with water.

Sometimes I feel like the old minister who preached baptism, baptism only, and baptism continually. A self-appointed committee finally asked him to preach on the text: "They will beat their swords into plowshares" (Isa. 2: 4). Surely, they thought, he couldn't think of a hint of baptism in that passage. They really wanted a change of diet.

Sunday came and he began his sermon: "Swords are made of steel. So are axes made of steel. In the winter we have to use axes to cut the ice when we baptize." And then he swung right into his discourse on baptism.

However,

> if we desire to follow the teaching and example of the New Testament, water baptism should be required for membership in His Church. . . . One does not become a Christian by simply being baptized. The New Testament makes it clear that there is only one saving response—that is faith. "For by grace you have been saved through faith" (Eph. 2:8). But this inner gate of entrance into the Church as the body of Christ is to be complemented by the visible gate of water baptism.[17]

Philip went right down into the water and baptized the wealthy, influential Ethiopian and welcomed him into the family of God. As the brand-new baby Christian rejoiced, praising God, and expressed the relief of his aching heart to all of his servants, chariot drivers, and caravaners, Philip was led away north to preach to others the unsearchable riches of Christ. But the Ethiopian official "went on his way rejoicing" (Acts 8:39). How unlike the rich young ruler who "went away sorrowful" (Matt. 19:22, KJV).

The Ethiopian eunuch, known as Indich, took the Good News with him into Ethiopia. This first Gentile convert told of Jesus until his country became a responsive harvest field for the kingdom of God. The prophecy of Ps. 68:31 (KJV) was fulfilled: "Ethiopia shall soon stretch out her hands unto God." Tradition says that the eunuch finally baptized the Candace or queen of Ethiopia. It is believed that the Coptic and Abyssinian churches yet today are lingering fruits of the Ethiopian eunuch's conversion.

Only God can see the real results from a few moments of witnessing to someone whose heart the Holy Spirit has prepared. Our old world needs men under orders—willing to be the right person at the right place at the right time, doing God's work in God's way. God plans a long way ahead of this present moment. Any fool can count the number of seeds in an apple; only God can count how many apples are in a seed!

Obedience to the promptings of the Spirit—that's where the action is!

At the conclusion of a rather lengthy sermon, a friend whispered to his neighbor in church: "Is the sermon finished?"

His neighbor thoughtfully replied: "No, my friend. The preacher is finished, but the sermon now must be worked out in our lives!"

Footnotes

Chapter 1

1. Myron S. Augsburger, *Quench Not the Spirit* (Scottdale, Pa.: Herald Press, 1961), p. 60.

2. Joseph H. Mayfield and Ralph Earle, *Beacon Bible Commentary* (Kansas City: Beacon Hill Press, 1965), 7:309.

3. William Sanford LaSor, *Church Alive* (Glendale, Calif.: Regal Books Division, G/L Publications, 1972), p. 75.

4. Louis H. Evans, *Life's Hidden Power* (Westwood, N.J.: Fleming H. Revell Co., 1958), p. 126.

5. J. W. Goodwin, *The Gospel for Our Age* (Kansas City: Nazarene Publishing House, n.d.), p. 165.

6. Augsburger, *Quench Not the Spirit*, p. 60.

7. William Barclay, *Fishers of Men* (Philadelphia: Westminster Press, 1966), p. 96.

8. *Worship in Song*, hymnal (Kansas City: Lillenas Publishing Co., 1972), p. 280.

Chapter 2

1. George Arthur Buttrick, ed., *The Interpreter's Bible* (New York: Abingdon Press, 1954), 9:55-56.

2. C. William Fisher in radio sermon, "All This—And Heaven Too! . . . and 'This' Means Healing," "Showers of Blessing" broadcast.

3. William Barclay, *The Acts of the Apostles*, The Daily Study Bible (Philadelphia: Westminster Press, 1953), p. 44.

4. Norman Vincent Peale, *Favorite Stories of Positive Faith* (Pawling, N.Y.: Foundation for Christian Living, 1974), pp. 46-47.

Chapter 3

1. William P. Barker, *They Stood Boldly* (Westwood, N.J.: Fleming H. Revell Co., 1967), p. 52.

2. Arnold E. Airhart, *Beacon Bible Expositions* (Kansas City: Beacon Hill Press of Kansas City, 1977), 5:66.

3. Ibid., p. 67.

4. Barker, *They Stood Boldly*, p. 52.

5. Charles W. Carter and Ralph Earle, *The Evangelical Commentary on the Acts of the Apostles* (Grand Rapids: Zondervan Publishing House, 1959), p. 77.

6. Barker, *They Stood Boldly*, p. 54.

7. Clyde E. Fant, Jr., and William M. Pinson, Jr., *Twenty Centuries of Great Preaching* (Waco, Tex.: Word Books, Publisher, 1971), 10:240-41.

8. *Worship in Song*, p. 1.

CHAPTER 4

1. Robert E. Maner, "Growing Pains," *Preacher's Magazine*, November, 1977.

2. Lyle Schaller, *The Decision-Makers* (Nashville: Abingdon, 1974), p. 58.

3. Ibid., p. 59.

4. Carl F. H. Henry, ed., *The Biblical Expositor* (Philadelphia: A. J. Holman Co., 1960), 3:198.

5. LaSor, *Church Alive*, p. 90.

6. William Barclay, *God's Young Church* (Philadelphia: Westminster Press, 1970), pp. 34-35.

7. Ray C. Stedman, *Birth of the Body* (Santa Ana, Calif.: Vision House Publications, 1974), p. 115.

8. Stuart Briscoe, *Living Dangerously* (Grand Rapids: Zondervan Publishing House, 1968), pp. 112-13.

9. J. Oswald Sanders, *Spiritual Leadership* (Chicago: Moody Press, 1967), p. 71.

10. Everett Lewis Cattell, *The Spirit of Holiness* (Grand Rapids: William B. Eerdmans Publishing Co., 1963), p. 74.

11. Fletcher Spruce, *Of Grasshoppers and Giants* (Kansas City: Beacon Hill Press of Kansas City, 1975), p. 23.

CHAPTER 5

1. E. Stanley Jones, *The Way to Power and Poise* (New York: Abingdon-Cokesbury Press, 1949), p. 119.

2. Buttrick, ed., *The Interpreter's Bible*, 9:96.

3. C. Roy Angell, *God's Gold Mines* (Nashville: Broadman Press, 1962), pp. 72-73.

4. Mayfield and Earle, *Beacon Bible Commentary*, 7:331.

5. Briscoe, *Living Dangerously*, pp. 108-9.

6. Buttrick, ed., *The Interpreter's Bible*, 9:103.

7. *Worship in Song*, p. 207.

8. Harold L. Fickett, Jr., *Profiles in Clay* (Los Angeles: Cowman Publishing Co., 1963), p. 146.

9. Frank E. Butterworth, *So Now He Speaks Again* (New York: Abingdon Press, 1963), p. 103.

CHAPTER 6

1. Barclay, *The Acts of the Apostles*, p. 63.

2. Stedman, *Birth of the Body*, p. 132.

3. Barker, *They Stood Boldly*, p. 65.

4. Ibid., p. 66.

5. Ibid.

6. Stedman, *Birth of the Body*, p. 132.

7. Bishop Festo Kivengere, *I Love Idi Amin* (Old Tappan, N.J.: Fleming H. Revell Co., 1977), p. 13.

8. George W. Truett, *The Salt of the Earth* (Grand Rapids: Wm. B. Eerdmans Publishing Co., 1949), p. 135.

9. Lloyd John Ogilvie, *Drumbeat of Love* (Waco, Tex.: Word Books, Publishers, 1976), pp. 101-2.

10. William J. Fallis, *Studies in Acts* (Nashville: Broadman Press, 1949), p. 48.

11. William M. Greathouse, *The Fullness of the Spirit* (Kansas City: Nazarene Publishing House, 1958), p. 89.

12. Halford E. Luccock, *Marching off the Map* (New York: Harper and Brothers, Publishers, 1952), pp. 110-11.

CHAPTER 7

1. E. M. Bounds, *Power Through Prayer* (Chicago: Moody Press, n.d.), p. 8.

2. Airhart, *Beacon Bible Expositions*, 5:96.

3. Edward E. Hinson, *Glory in the Church* (New York: Thomas Nelson, Publishers, 1975), p. 30.

4. Henry Jacobsen, *The Acts Then and Now* (Wheaton, Ill.: Victor Books, a division of Scripture Press Publications, 1973), p. 68.

5. Ogilvie, *Drumbeat of Love*, p. 107.

6. John T. Seamands, *On Tiptoe with Love* (Kansas City: Beacon Hill Press of Kansas City, 1971), p. 29.

7. Augsburger, *Quench Not the Spirit*, p. 71.

8. Ogilvie, *Drumbeat of Love*, p. 110.

9. Luccock, *Marching off the Map*, p. 27.

10. Charles L. Allen, *Prayer Changes Things* (Westwood, N.J.: Fleming H. Revell Co., 1964), p. 33.

CHAPTER 8

1. *Nuggets of Good News* (Lincoln, Neb.: Back to the Bible Publishers, 1950), p. 26.

2. Helen Temple, "Ready—Can Mean the Unexpected," *World Mission*, September, 1977.

3. D. James Kennedy, *Evangelism Explosion* (Wheaton, Ill.: Tyndale House Publishers, 1970), preface.

4. Jones, *Power and Poise*, p. 153.

5. Mrs. Gordon T. Olsen, "Stay Close." President's Paragraphs, *World Mission*, issue unidentified.

6. Barclay, *The Acts of the Apostles*, p. 70.

7. Vance Havner, *The Best of Vance Havner* (Old Tappan, N.J.: Fleming H. Revell Co., 1969), p. 24.

8. Ogilvie, *Drumbeat of Love*, p. 112.

9. Havner, *Best of Havner*, pp. 24-25.

10. William F. Kerr, gen. ed., *Ministers' Research Service* (Wheaton, Ill.: Tyndale House Publishers, 1972), p. 495.

11. Ogilvie, *Drumbeat of Love*, p. 112.

12. Ibid., p. 122.

13. Ibid., p. 123.

14. Temple, "Ready."

15. W. E. Sangster, *They Met at Calvary* (New York: Abingdon Press, 1956), p. 105.

16. Marcus Bach, *The Will to Believe* (Englewood Cliffs, N.J.: Prentice-Hall, 1955), pp. 180-81.

17. Richard E. Howard, *Newness of Life* (Kansas City: Beacon Hill Press of Kansas City, 1975), p. 123.

Bibliography

Airhart, Arnold E. *Beacon Bible Expositions*, vol. 5. Kansas City: Beacon Hill Press of Kansas City, 1977.

Alford, Henry. *The New Testament for English Readers.* Chicago: Moody Press, n.d.

Allen, Charles L. *Prayer Changes Things.* Westwood, N.J.: Fleming H. Revell Co. , 1964.

Angell, C. Roy. *God's Gold Mines.* Nashville: Broadman Press, 1962.

Augsburger, Myron S. *Quench Not the Spirit.* Scottdale, Pa.: Herald Press, 1961.

Bach, Marcus. *The Will to Believe.* Englewood Cliffs, N.J.: Prentice-Hall, 1955.

Barclay, William. *Fishers of Men.* Philadelphia: Westminster Press, 1966.

———. *God's Young Church.* Philadelphia: Westminster Press, 1970.

———. *The Acts of the Apostles,* The Daily Study Bible. Philadelphia: Westminster Press, 1953.

Barker, William P. *They Stood Boldly.* Westwood, N.J.: Fleming H. Revell Co., 1967.

Benson, Joseph. *Benson's Commentary,* vol. 4. New York: T. Mason and G. Lane, 1839.

Blackwood, Andrew Watterson. *Expository Preaching for Today.* New York: Abingdon Press, 1953.

———. *Planning a Year's Pulpit Work.* New York: Abingdon Press, 1952.

Blair, Edward P. *The Acts and Apocalyptic Literature.* New York: Abingdon-Cokesbury Press, 1956.

Bounds, E. M. *Power Through Prayer.* Chicago: Moody Press, n.d.

Briscoe, Stuart. *Living Dangerously.* Grand Rapids: Zondervan Publishing House, 1968.

Bruce, F. F. *Commentary on the Book of the Acts,* The New

International Commentary on the New Testament. Grand Rapids: Wm. B. Eerdmans Publishing Co., 1976.

Butterworth, Frank E. *So Now He Speaks Again*. New York: Abingdon Press, 1963.

Buttrick, George Arthur, ed. *The Interpreter's Bible*, vol. 9. New York: Abingdon Press, 1954.

Carter, Charles W., and Earle, Ralph. *The Evangelical Commentary on the Acts of the Apostles.* Grand Rapids: Zondervan Publishing House, 1959.

Carver, William Owen. *The Acts of the Apostles*. Nashville: Broadman Press, 1916.

Cattell, Everett Lewis. *The Spirit of Holiness*. Grand Rapids: William B. Eerdmans Publishing Co., 1963.

Clarke, Adam. *Clarke's Commentary*, vol. 5. New York: Abingdon Press, n.d.

Davidson, F., ed. *The New Bible Commentary*. Grand Rapids: Wm. B. Eerdmans Publishing Co., 1958.

Ellicott, Charles John. *A Bible Commentary for English Readers*, vol. 7. London: Cassell and Co., n.d.

Evans, Louis H. *Life's Hidden Power*. Westwood, N.J.: Fleming H. Revell Co., 1958.

Fallis, William J. *Studies in Acts*. Nashville: Broadman Press, 1949.

Fant, Clyde E., Jr., and Pinson, William H., Jr. *Twenty Centuries of Great Preaching*, vol. 10. Waco, Tex.: Word Books, Publishers, 1971.

Fickett, Harold L., Jr. *Profiles in Clay*. Los Angeles: Cowman Publishing Co., 1963.

Fisher, C. William. "All This—And Heaven Too! . . . and 'This' Means Healing." Radio sermon, "Showers of Blessing" broadcast.

Goodwin, J. W. *The Gospel for Our Age*. Kansas City: Nazarene Publishing House, n.d.

Greathouse, William M. *The Fullness of the Spirit*. Kansas City: Nazarene Publishing House, 1958.

Havner, Vance. *The Best of Vance Havner*. Old Tappan, N.J.: Fleming H. Revell Co., 1969.

Henry, Carl F. H., ed. *The Biblical Expositor*, vol. 3. Philadelphia: A. J. Holman Co., 1960.

Henry, Matthew. *Matthew Henry's Commentary*. Edited by Leslie F. Church. Grand Rapids: Zondervan Publishing House, 1961.

Hervey, A. C. *The Acts of the Apostles*, vol. 1. The Pulpit Commentary, edited by H. D. M. Spence and Joseph S. Exell. London: Funk and Wagnalls Co., 1908.

Hinson, Edward E. *Glory in the Church*. New York: Thomas Nelson, Publishers, 1975.

Howard, Richard E. *Newness of Life*. Kansas City: Beacon Hill Press of Kansas City, 1975.

Jacobsen, Henry. *The Acts Then and Now*. Wheaton, Ill.: Victor Books, a division of Scripture Press Publications, 1973.

Jones, E. Stanley. *Growing Spiritually*. New York: Abingdon Press, 1953.

———. *How to Be a Transformed Person*. New York: Abingdon-Cokesbury Press, 1951.

———. *The Way to Power and Poise*. New York: Abingdon-Cokesbury Press, 1949.

Kennedy, D. James. *Evangelism Explosion*. Wheaton, Ill.: Tyndale House Publishers, 1970.

Kerr, William F., gen. ed. *Ministers' Research Service*. Wheaton, Ill.: Tyndale House Publishers, 1972.

Kivengere, Bishop Festo. *I Love Idi Amin*. Old Tappan, N.J.: Fleming H. Revell Co., 1977.

LaSor, William Sanford. *Church Alive*. Glendale, Calif.: Regal Books Division, G/L Publications, 1972.

———. *Great Personalities of the New Testament*. Westwood, N.J.: Fleming H. Revell Co., 1961.

Lockyer, Herbert. *All the Prayers of the Bible*. Grand Rapids: Zondervan Publishing House, 1959.

Luccock, Halford E. *Marching off the Map*. New York: Harper and Brothers, Publishers, 1952.

Maner, Robert E. "Growing Pains," *Preacher's Magazine*, November, 1977.

Mayfield, Joseph H., and Earle, Ralph. *Beacon Bible Commentary*, vol. 7. Kansas City: Beacon Hill Press, 1965.

Morgan, G. Campbell. *The Acts of the Apostles*. Westwood, N.J.: Fleming H. Revell Co., 1924.

Nuggets of Good News. Lincoln, Neb.: Back to the Bible Publishers, 1950.

Ogilvie, Lloyd John. *Drumbeat of Love*. Waco, Tex.: Word Books, Publishers, 1976.

Olsen, Mrs. Gordon T. "Stay Close." President's Paragraphs, *World Mission*, issue unidentified.

Peale, Norman Vincent. *Favorite Stories of Positive Faith*. Pawling, N.Y.: Foundation for Christian Living, 1974.

Robertson, Archibald Thomas. *Word Pictures of the New Testament*, vol. 3. Nashville: Broadman Press, 1930.

Sanders, J. Oswald. *Spiritual Leadership*. Chicago: Moody Press, 1967.

Sangster, W. E. *They Met at Calvary*. New York: Abingdon Press, 1956.

Schaller, Lyle. *The Decision-Makers*. Nashville: Abingdon, 1974.

Seamands, John T. *On Tiptoe with Love*. Kansas City: Beacon Hill Press of Kansas City, 1971.

Smith, Roy L. *Making a Go of Life*. New York: Abingdon Press, 1958.

Spruce, Fletcher. *Of Grasshoppers and Giants*. Kansas City: Beacon Hill Press of Kansas City, 1975.

———. *When God Comes*. Kansas City: Beacon Hill Press, 1950.

Stedman, Ray C. *Birth of the Body*. Santa Ana, Calif.: Vision House Publications, 1974.

Temple, Helen. "Ready—Can Mean the Unexpected." *World Mission*, September, 1977.

Thomas, W. H. Griffith. *Outline Studies in the Acts of the Apostles*. Grand Rapids: Wm. B. Eerdmans Publishing Co., 1956.

Tournier, Paul. *Guilt and Grace*. New York: Harper and Row, Publishers, 1962.

Truett, George W. *The Salt of the Earth*. Grand Rapids: Wm. B. Eerdmans Publishing Co., 1949.

Unger, Merrill F. *Unger's Bible Dictionary*. Chicago: Moody Press, 1957.

Worship in Song. Kansas City: Lillenas Publishing Co., 1972.

Yocum, Dale M. *Conformed to Christ*. Cincinnati: Revivalist Press, 1962.